Charlene, thank you for reading my book; I appreciate it! Many Blessings

Lofty Dreams with Broken Wings

LOFTY DREAMS WITH BROKEN WINGS

An Exhortation of Love, Healing, and Restoration

ANGELA DRAUGHN

XULON PRESS

Xulon Press
2301 Lucien Way #415
Maitland, FL 32751
407.339.4217
www.xulonpress.com

Paperback ISBN-13: 978-1-6628-4561-1
Ebook ISBN-13: 978-1-6628-4562-8

I dedicate this book to my heavenly Father, without whom I would not have survived the things that broke my wings.

Acknowledgments

My Buffalo Soldiers

To My Buffalos

Pastor John Jenkins, Bishop T.D. Jakes, Sarah Moore, Darlene Williams, Nicole Clough, Rosita and Isaias Palacios, Elizabeth and Inmar Conde, Donald and Melissa Dixon, Darrell and Letitia Dixon, Ivie Dixon, Tina Hyman, Kenia Cooper, Nicole Clough, Matthew Clough, Brian Buchanan, Shaundale Rena, Janice and Roland Smith, Barbara Thompson, Tass Thompson, Diane Simms, Angie Murphy, Kim R. Ford, Tiffany Williams, Matt "Ted" Miller, Dr. Irvin Moore, Deirdre Neighbors, Ashanti Narce, LaShawn D. Montague, Gloria Vest, Darci Henderson, Kevin Green, David Bullock, Angela Moore, Delores Crowder, Rhonda Neal, Anthony Wheeler, Dr. Patricia Frazier, Ruby, Max, and Chip Draughn, my nieces, nephews, cousins, coworkers, and all students I had the pleasure to teach...Thank you!

Contents

Author's Note

I love birds, everything about them—their colors, their habits, their beauty, their song, but most importantly, their freedom. When I watch them fly, I marvel at the glory of their gift. They get to see the world from high places. Once asked if I could be any other creature other than human, what would I be, hands down, my answer was a bird. In the Bible, birds were messengers from heaven. The dove and raven all played a role in communicating a directive from God. To me, they are the very essence of beauty and grace until you see the heartbreaking sight of one with a broken wing. How the bird suffered the injury may never be known but helping it fly again is the challenge.

Though a bird can survive a broken wing, it will never fly and thrive again without restoration. There is, however, an improved chance the bird can fly again with proper professional care. The parallels between birds not being able to fly and what kept me from soaring were very thought-provoking. After years of suffering, my sister-in-law asked me what kept me from fulfilling my purpose. I said, "Sis, I have lofty dreams but broken wings." It was this conversation that stirred my heart to write this book. I realize that many people are experiencing a desire to do better but, for some reason, remain stuck in a rut that, unbeknownst to them, may have everything to do with some area of brokenness in their consciousness.

This brokenness could show up in relationships, finances, personal surroundings, church, and even the workforce. For me, it showed up in every area. Like many, I did not realize it. I had no clue how to decipher what it meant or why I had experienced it. I knew I had dreams, and I wanted to do something purposeful with my life. I just did not realize that the path to purpose could be filled with bumps, bruises, crooked roads, detours, peaks, valleys, droughts, and famine. As a child, all I had ever known about growing up was dreaming big, getting a job, paying bills, being successful, accumulating things, having a family, retiring, etc. Life quickly had some reality checks for me.

As I got older and started entering the workforce, I discovered many people dragging their feet through the office, barely making it. They were determined to hold on until they retired, no matter how long it took them to obtain that goal. They were stuck in a rut, a routine, and a lackluster space in their lives that caused them to succumb to business as usual. I'll never get that way, I thought. I'll always push the envelope, seek new goals, reach for higher heights, and soar to places only seen in my dreams. I had a plan, a timeline, goals—and then life happened. The plan was obscure, the timeline was blown, and my goals took a back burner to discover the true existence of Christ. The joy of learning about Jesus filled my heart with glee until I met some of the ones who represented Him.

I had often heard people say they did not want to go to church because of "Church Folk." What an awful thing to think about the children of God. To me, the people who said such things were just looking for excuses not to believe and to continue living in their sinful ways, but then the days came when I was tired, tried, and burned out. Then, I began to understand how a person who loves God could become a church cliché, with no passion in relationships, no fire in your prayer life, judgmental of others, falling asleep during service, thinking to yourself: please for the love of God—wrap this up. This book will take you through the journey of salvation, success, pride, tragedy, humility, repentance, redemption, restoration, and triumph—the human experiences that grow our faith in God. I present to you, *Lofty Dreams with Broken Wings*.

Seeds of Greatness

"Angela is a good student,
but she talks entirely too much."

—Mrs. Thompson, first-grade teacher

Across the world, people from all walks of life visit Washington, DC, to see the glory of the cherry trees in full blossom. The beautiful, showy flowers whisper the promise of better days as winter gives way to spring. The birds sing, the wind blows, and people enthusiastically come out of their seasonal hibernation. Understanding the lure of the trees may be a mystery to some, but to me, it represents confidence, faithfulness, strength, and resilience. These trees have survived storms, riots, pests, droughts, and even a pandemic, just to name a few. They have remained beautiful despite environmental changes and faithfully show the world their greatness at just the right moment. As a Washingtonian, I look forward to that time of the year. It is the thing I love most about my beautiful city.

Though there are very few other places I would want to make my home, North Carolina will always have a special place in my heart. I spent some of the best times of my life there at my grandmother's home in Washington, NC. Running outside barefoot, catching lightning bugs, making mud pies, climbing trees, and laying in the grass, watching clouds was exhilarating to a child like me: a true lover of the great outdoors. When I was one, I climbed on the dining room table my mother set for breakfast and tried to drink a cup of scalding hot coffee, which left me with second and third-degree burns on my chest. My scars were so bad I needed around-the-clock care to keep me from infecting my wounds. My working parents could not afford to hire a nurse, so they made the tough decision to let me live in North Carolina with my maternal grandparents.

My grandmother, Olga, was a person of great prudence despite only having a third-grade education. At the tender age of thirteen, she married my grandfather, Jack, when he was only seventeen with an eighth-grade education. Together, they raised nine children, with the fifth one being my mother, Barbara. When I moved to North Carolina from Washington, DC, I lived in a house with empty-nesters. My grandparents and my great-grandmother, Ida, showered me with love, attention, and anything else I wanted. They treated me like gold. In their minds, I was precious, beautiful, smart, and very capable. They never failed to encourage me with those words.

Children raised by older people are often considered old souls, a child wise far beyond their age. Such was the case with me. Life was filled with teachable moments, and I had farmers of great wisdom sowing into my field of potential. One such time was after I finished eating an apple. I asked my grandmother about the seeds in it, and she told me if I'd plant the seeds in the ground, they would grow into a tree, producing the same kind of apples. I decided to give it a try. I took the seeds from my apple and planted them. I would go outside and water my patch of dirt and dream about my apple tree. Not long after I planted those seeds, we moved from Chocowinity, NC, to Washington, NC. Though I was sad that I could not see my tree grow, my attention was quickly diverted as I discovered our new home had barns in the backyard.

To help me adjust to the move, my grandmother took her old furniture and put it in one of the barns, which became my clubhouse. I quickly made friends, and the neighborhood children and I would play in it, pretending we were watching TV, but not without charging them a nickel entrance fee. Although I wanted to stay home and play in my clubhouse, I had to go to school, quickly developing a love for reading. I learned how to sound words out and how to spell them. I would tell my grandmother about my day and then play by myself, pretending to have a classroom by mimicking my teachers.

Teaching my class and smelling steak, potatoes, gravy, fresh string beans, and homemade biscuits are among my fondest memories of my grandmother. In the South, the front porch often solidified a sense of community. We would sit and snap string beans, shooting the breeze with neighbors, often over a glass of tea. Things were simpler then because we loved each other. Many think having more money is the answer to all problems in today's world, and money does answer many things, but being a child in a household with empty-nesters was the richest moment of my life. Whenever my mother or one of my aunts or uncles would come home to visit their parents, I would be there to experience that love from them as well.

The greatness of community collaboration filled me and significantly impacted my life. My grandmother was such a beautiful person and had the heart to serve. I emulated everything she did, but I did not know her life came with challenges. I remember asking her for help with my reading, and she told me she could not read. Quietly, I pondered an answer and lovingly said, "Don't worry, Big Momma. I will show you how to read." Every day, I took a lesson home and sat with her. I taught her how to sound the words out, and she would learn as I learned. We sat in the kitchen as her biscuits cooked in the oven and bonded over the words of a book. "You are going to be a teacher one day," she said to me lovingly. "Yes, Ma'am," I replied.

Big Momma, as she was affectionately known, planted that seed of greatness in me, and I took those words and hid them in my heart. I did not care that she could not read. I wanted to be just like her when I grew up. At the tender age of six, my grandmother got sick and had surgery that left her unable to care for me. Though she wanted me to stay anyway, my mother thought it best for me to join my family in Washington, DC, so reluctantly, I moved.

Living in DC was a big adjustment because butterflies, birds, dogs, church, and a small community of family and friends filled my prior life. The big city felt cold and uncaring. I went from hearing birds chirping to sirens in the street. Everything about the city scared me. The concrete walls, the loud sounds, the vernacular of the community, the sight of broken glass, men with alcohol in brown paper bags hanging on the street corners, and the stench of trash and urine were all too much for my senses. I was even frustrated about leaving my five-bedroom home for a small two-bedroom apartment I shared with my siblings. Though I love my mother dearly, I must admit that I was not the nicest child because my grandparents had spoiled me. There was a certain comfort to be had in a sheltered environment.

Added to my difficult transition was my tendencies to have phobias exacerbated by the woes of city living.

When my mother was pregnant with me, she fell up the stairs on her stomach and went into labor shortly thereafter. I often told her I believe that fall contributed to my fear of heights. For years, I was terrified of high places, especially climbing stairs; I always felt like I would fall. On a subconscious level, I think that may have something to do with why it took me so long to write this book. I guess I was afraid of the possibility of where something like this would take me. I was often just looking for affirmation, a hint that I really could do it.

I did not realize that not everyone would believe in me and that to be great, I had to believe in myself. Sometimes we look to celebrities and people of certain notoriety as our only examples of great people. The truth is, everyone has that potential. My family was great because they could love you beyond your faults to your core. That type of comfort and love felt terrific.

When I started school in DC, I missed the simplicity of my small town in Carolina because people were different in DC. Because I had a third-degree burn, the students were tough on me. There were very few days when people did not ridicule my accent. They taunted me by calling me "Country Time." As I got older, I began to love that I was a little bit country and a little bit rock and roll. I had the best of both worlds. Though I loved to talk, I would only open up to my good friends. I discovered that communicating was a gift, but any gift left unopened could not be genuinely appreciated. The thoughts of the unopened gift remind me of a lesson I learned as a child.

One Christmas, I got up before anyone else and went to open my toys. There was a van with my name on it, but it did not have anything in it; it was just a boring van. I looked over at my sister's van, and it had all kinds of gadgets to it, so I switched the names on the gifts because I wanted what she had. When my mother got up and saw me playing with her toy, she swapped it back. I still remember the attitude I had because I did not like my gift. It was plain, and I felt my sister's present was much better. I can still see the annoyance on my mother's face as she watched my ungrateful attitude. She then began to show me my gift.

Hidden on top of my van was a compartment with several clothes for my doll—a much better gift for me and very befitting of my personality. I knew I had done something wrong because of how my mother responded to my attitude, and even though she never verbally gave me the lesson, life handed it to me. Some people have gifts obvious to everyone, and we think those gifts are great and often covet them. There are also those whose gifts are subtle, often hidden from plain sight, but brilliantly executed with precision, without which many things would never be accomplished. Greatness is uncovering the valuable treasure within you and presenting those treasures back to the Creator for His glory. ("We now have this light shining in our hearts, but we ourselves are like fragile clay jars containing this great treasure. This makes it clear that our great power is from God, not from ourselves." (2 Cor. 4:7, NLT)

It wasn't until I was in college that I began to cultivate my gift of communication. I talked a lot, but I also had something to say. As much as I enjoy expressing myself, writing this book was one of the most difficult things I have ever accomplished. Partly because my life was filled with many peaks and valleys, mostly because I lacked the healing, discipline, and focus I needed to achieve this goal. Therefore, I sought to unveil why I could not sit still enough to write, which led me down a path of self-examination.

Since childhood, I knew I was different. On the one hand, I was extremely introverted, but on the other hand, I could be the life of the party. These conflicts in my personality made my teenage years almost unbearable. For one year in middle school, my mother moved to North Carolina to live with my grandparents. I was sad to leave my best friend, Darlene, but I was delighted to be back with my grandmother. Since the town only had one middle school, the chances of being taught by the same teachers who had taught my mother and her siblings were high; such was the case with me.

I was assigned to a teacher who had once taught my rambunctious uncles; needless to say; she did not like me from the start. Throughout my school days, she would make offensive remarks to me, such as, "I don't know how you do things in the big city, but that's not how we do things here." She would refer to me as a city slicker. I was twelve; I had no idea what a city slicker was. Despite the difficult relationship I had with this adult, I managed to make some good friends in my class. They helped make the move back to North Carolina much better.

During the winter, I got sick with the flu and stayed out of school for about two weeks. Upon my return, no one in my class wanted to talk to me or sit with me. I was alone and confused. After a while, my friends came back to me, but it was obvious my teacher did not want me in the class.

One day, someone played a practical joke on a student in class, and I started laughing. The teacher immediately thought it was me. As a teenager, I went through this stage where I thought everything was funny—not just funny but falling rolling on the floor, laughing funny. No matter how much I tried to explain to her that I did not play the joke, she accused me and made a special trip to tell my mother what she thought I had done, along with other observations. I was tremendously hurt when I found out adults could lie. My teacher's implicit bias about me caused her to see me in the light of a stereotypical city person coming to destroy the South's good, wholesome values. Her attitude toward me caused me great harm. It made me feel rejected.

When I got older and returned to North Carolina, one of my former classmates told me our teacher told everyone in class not to speak to me or hang with me because I was a bad influence on them, and they would end up just like me. When I told my mother how the teacher had treated me, she apologized for disciplining me and wished I would have told her what was going on in my class.

When you live in a loving and supportive environment at home, it's easy to expect that same type of love from other people you encounter. Every child can do great things and be great human beings, but sometimes it is the adult who breaks them. This often happens when grown-ups are not cognizant of the tone, words, and actions they use when dealing with the frailty of children. Inadvertently, I have said harsh things under the guise of being brutally honest, but you should never present anything brutal to a child. Their fragile minds are in no emotional state to handle all doses of reality, and most adults aren't either. Learning that delicate balance between correction and a harsh approach is vitally important to the preservation of their self-worth.

My teacher had spent a year trying to anchor me into failure with the words she spoke about me. After spending a year in her class, I missed the days of DC. I was happy to learn that we were moving back, but lurking over my head was a dark cloud filled with one of the most horrific things that could happen to a child in school, bullying. I had made friends with a girl in my classroom. One day, this girl drew a picture of a distorted figure of a grotesque lady with a face full of polka dots, supposedly representing my acne. Suddenly, the students were snickering. I asked everyone what they were laughing at and to my surprise, the person I thought was my friend put my name on the paper to poke fun at my skin. My self-esteem was already low because of my burn and seventh-grade experience, but this attack was a tremendous blow to my internal image.

Barely hanging on, I poured my energy into running. I had dreams of going to the Olympics. My proudest moment was running track back in North Carolina, where I won a race with Michael Jordan in the audience at Chapel Hill. Running track allowed me to clear my head and forget about my troubles. I worked hard to increase my speed in preparation for an indoor track meet. My hair was not long, my face was covered with pimples, and I did not have the best track shoes, but I was determined to win.

Just as it was my turn to run, the coach told me he was replacing me with another student. I sat there that whole track meeting sunken. The girl was prettier than I was, so I assumed that was his reason because he did not give me a chance. I sat in the stands, watching her lose my 100-yard dash. Apparently, he saw the sadness in my eyes because privately, he came to me and told me he was wrong for doing it, and it would not happen again. However, his apologies meant nothing to me. To have once been called Wilma Rudolph was a tremendous seed of greatness, but when my track coach did that to me, I quit the team and began to suffocate under the weeds of self-doubt, rejection, and just thoughts of not being good enough to belong in this world, so I contemplated suicide.

My saving grace was church. The messages seemed to be tailor-made just for me. When they asked us to give our hearts to God, I went to the altar but could not stop crying. The evangelist sent me back to my seat because I could not get myself together. I tried to stop, but my emotions were raw. I did not know how to contain the heaviness in my heart. I decided to learn about God by reading the Bible stories my mother had bought us. These books were the illustrated Word of God from Genesis to Revelation.

Learning about God gave me the strength I needed to make it out of middle school. In the ninth grade, I had great teachers at Anacostia Senior High who saw my talent. I joined the Junior Reserved Officer Training Corps (JROTC), entered a humanities program, played in the band, became a drama club member, and had finally begun to see some slight positive changes in my life. The one thing that remained the same were the students I had in the middle school also attended my high school. Initially, I wanted to attend Duke Ellington School of the Arts, but because we were on a tight budget, the bus fare and other possible incidental fees made that dream unobtainable. So I went to my neighborhood school, where I could feel the safety of my brother. Going to school with him was comforting because he was a handsome, popular athlete, and that provided me with a level of protection and kept me from suffering as much as I could have. However, I still never felt confident around some people.

I can remember going into classes and people talking about how ugly my face and hair were, but the boys complimented the shape of my body. In my mind, this told me that perhaps having a beautiful body was the only thing I had going for me. Those words were like shards of glass to my ego. I honor my mother for helping me through those hard times. She always felt a sense of sorrow when it came to my scar but worked diligently to help me find the courage I needed to survive. She did not shield me from it but, rather, equipped me to overcome it.

For years, my mother would tell me how beautiful I was, but it was not her voice that I heard through the halls of my school. It was the pretty girls and the handsome boys. They were the ones laughing at my looks, hair, and clothes. They made it difficult for me to hold my head up high. I recall how difficult it was to look in the mirror, even to comb my hair after gym class, especially if the pretty girls were waiting behind me. One day my mother noticed that I always had my head down and could not look in the mirror. She made me hold my head up, and while standing behind me, she spoke words of affirmation into my life. Though it was a difficult concept to accept, eventually, it worked. If you are reading this book and you have a child struggling with self-image issues, I say to you, "Your words will be nourishment to their soul."

In any great garden, there will always be things to threaten the existence of your plant. It wasn't until I started gardening that I got a full understanding of the process of sowing seed and reaping harvest. Learning the role soil, earthworms, rain, and sun play in your plant's growth is quite profound and similar to life. No matter how hard my mother encouraged me with her words, someone was always there to try and choke them with their hateful agenda.

Jesus spoke about the parable of the farmer scattering seed in the Gospel of Luke 8:4–8, NLT:

> One day, Jesus told a story in the form of a parable to a large crowd that had gathered from many towns to hear him: A farmer went out to plant his seed. As he scattered it across his field, some seed fell on a footpath, where it was stepped on, and the birds ate it. Other seed fell among rocks. It began to grow, but the plant soon wilted and died for lack of

> moisture. Other seed fell among thorns that grew up with it and choked out the tender plants. Still, other seed fell on fertile soil. This seed grew and produced a crop that was a hundred times as much as had been planted!" When he had said this, he called out, "Anyone with ears to hear should listen and understand."

The days and nights I cried, struggling to see my worth, were just me watering my precious seed. Many children grow up in homes where maybe their teachers tell them they are great, but a frustrated parent may tell them they are stupid. I have heard parents curse their own children with their words. Obviously, the parent had been broken as well. No child dreams of growing up to be a bum. No, if you ask a child what they want to be when they grow up, they tell you something lofty. Navigating through the terrains of those dreams in a toxic environment is detrimental to the psyche. My pastor used to tell us that *hurt people, hurt people*. Unfortunately, the vicious cycle of that pain creates generational hardships and unhealthy patterns destined to be repeated until someone decides to take another path.

For me, joining JROTC was a detour off the path of harmful words. The class taught me the importance of leadership. All my life, I displayed some leadership skills. While in elementary, I was captain of the school guard traffic safety patrols. I marched in the Cherry Blossom Parade, leading the school patrols in perfect formation. My leadership skills earned me an invitation to the Washington football team's training camp, which used to be located in Carlisle, Pennsylvania. There I stood in the cafeteria, excited about being in Pennsylvania, but I hadn't a clue as to who the players were. Suddenly a tall man asked me if I wanted to take a picture with him. I said, "Okay."

All the boys around me were saying, "She's taking a picture with blah blah blah . . ." That's all I heard for years until the photo got lost during a move; I did not have a clue as to who picked me out of the crowd to take a picture with him. Some thirty years later, it dawned on me that I had taken a picture with Art Monk. When I finally figured it out, I laughed at myself. I looked unimpressed in that picture because I did not know I was standing beside a future Hall of Famer and one of the greatest wide receivers of all time. Life is peculiar that way. Often, we assign "a value" to people because we do not know who they are, and perhaps on a subconscious level, we assign "a value" to ourselves because we do not know who we are, either.

Learning to lead at a young age and being rewarded for it made it easy to excel at JROTC. In fact, six months into the program, I was promoted to a staff sergeant and served on the executive committee with all the other officers. My teacher and mentor, Colonel Charles Lawson, was good at recognizing greatness. He developed that potential in me to such a degree that I became the highest-ranking girl at my school, the second command of my battalion, and the second-highest-ranking girl in the DC Public Schools' JROTC program.

One year during our city competition, I had to step up and serve as the company leader during a citywide competition in front of Mayor Marion Barry and all the city officials. I had not practiced leading the battalion, but I was ready because Colonel Lawson had prepared me to walk in the confidence of my leadership. The boys in my school challenged my authority, but on that day, I gave it everything I had, and though we came in third place, I was immensely proud of myself. I felt I could do anything.

That would have been my proudest moment in JROTC had it not been for the year prior when I was selected to meet and escort Astronaut Colonel Frederick Gregory, an alumnus of my high school, Anacostia Senior High. This gentleman was a NASA challenger pilot and nephew of the great Dr. Charles Drew. Meeting Colonel Gregory stirred something in me, as space exploration was something I grew up loving. In the seventh grade, I created an art project depicting the solar system, and it was chosen to be displayed in the mall for the whole town to see. After escorting Colonel Gregory, news reporters were running behind me to get an interview. "What has this meant to you?" they asked. "He has inspired me; he makes me want to be an astronaut," I answered.

Some of my classmates and friends laughed at me because I had that dream, so I hid my desire. Though I was terribly afraid of heights, I knew I would one day have to get over my fear, but I had no idea how to do so. I remember going to the Air and Space Museum in elementary school and being afraid to climb the steps, and I heard my teachers talking about me. "If she is like this now, can you imagine her when she gets older," they whispered to each other. Something about those words cut me deeply. Was I destined to be afraid of high places?

Years ago, I probably would have answered this question, yes, if it had not been for the great musician James Brown. Darlene and I concocted a plan to go see James perform at the former Post Office Pavilion in Downtown DC on New Year's Eve. She told her mother she was spending the night with me, and I told my mother I was spending the night with her, and we set off to see him perform. Oh, the fun we had until our eyes grew weary. We were seventeen, after all, and the bus was about to make its last trip. We did not realize it would only take us to the beginning of the Sousa Bridge. This bridge was the Pennsylvania Avenue connection from the White House to the east of the river. Since I grew up on the street connecting Pennsylvania Avenue, I had to catch that bus to get home.

When we discovered we'd partied with James Brown one song too many, we faced two choices: call our parents and tell them we had lied or cross that bridge. This old bridge crossing the Potomac River was poorly lit, and when cars drove by, you could feel the bridge move. It was in desperate need of repair. I was tired, cold, and had no money. Calling my mother collect at 1:00 a.m. (there were no cellphones back then) to tell her what I had done was not an option for me. It was my senior year in high school, and I did not want to miss out on all the senior events because I had lost my mother's trust.

Darlene offered to hold my hand and help me across the bridge. Little did she know the drama that would accompany her request. As all the bus passengers began their journey across the bridge, I stood there, screaming and crying from sheer terror. "Come on," Darlene beckoned. She pulled my hand, and I dug my feet in because fear paralyzed me. Eventually, she threatened to leave me, and that convinced me to move. I took slow, agonizing steps, each one more devastating than the other. I finally made it across—toes frozen, face cold, and knees shaking—but I had conquered my greatest fear: heights. I went home and told my mother I could not sleep. Darlene told her mother the same thing, and we agreed never to do that again.

I lay in my bed, trembling. We were blessed to have made it home that night. Unfortunately, not everyone shared our fate. Someone had strangled a young girl in the stairwells of the Pavilion not far from where we were standing. We were not sure how she got there or even if her parents knew she was out that night, but when we found this out, we were incredibly grateful for God's mercy even though our lies had put us in grave danger.

The Sousa Bridge had become a bridge over troubled waters. Everything about that night—the energy in the crowds, the bottle-throwing, the fights, and the bus not going over the bridge—could have crushed us and snuffed out every dream we ever had because of our bad decisions. Life lessons are not meant to keep us from growing. They are beacons of light to show us the way when times get dark. Amazingly enough, my lessons that night became my blessings as I was healed from my height phobia and my desire to lie to my mother. My path to greatness started as a mere seed but had the potential to develop into something substantial. Each experience provided me with the water, weeding, sunshine, and fertilizer I needed to help them grow.

Pathfinders

"I skate to where the puck is going to be, not where it has been." —Wayne Gretzky

It was the summer of '86, and the humidity was unusual even for Washington. I had recently graduated from high school, and I had no plan. I worked as a sales associate for a women's clothing store, but I wanted more. During the four years I spent in high school, I assumed I'd join the Air Force. Colonel Charles Lawson encouraged me to go to Howard University on a nursing scholarship, but all I wanted to do was find my own path. I gave him some half-wit excuse about my plans, but I believe he knew I was not completely honest with him. I was afraid to tell him I did not pass the Air Force test, and my SAT scores were not high enough to get into Howard. With all the potential I had growing up, I experienced a sense of loss by those two blows.

On my way home from my job at the mall, I saw a flier at the bus stop. It was an advertisement about a program recruiting DC residents to get free bank teller training. I thought, *A career in banking; I can do that.* I was accepted into the program and got a job at a bank in DC. I managed to keep my job at the clothing store by reducing my hours to part-time. That allowed me to buy professional clothing at a considerable discount. People always told me to dress for the position I wanted to be in, but no one ever said not to tell the boss of my aspirations for her job.

My bank manager was a young woman who seemed to have it out for me, partly because of my "fancy" clothes and perhaps because the male customers would bring me flowers, to which my boss said under her breath, "No one has ever brought me flowers." I can recall the time she came to me and threw a number on my desk. Using a snarky tone, she said, "I am not your personal secretary." I did not understand what she was talking about until I realized a gentleman I served called her and asked her to give me his telephone number. As the youngest person on my team, I was flattered, that is until her piercing eyes wiped that smile off my face. From that point on, it seemed as if she was continually auditing my drawer—lurking, waiting for one mistake.

An owner of a popular cookie shop had come to bring me a sample of his latest cookies. From that day on, my goose was cooked. It was the banking world's busiest day, Friday, August 1: the perfect storm, a bank teller's nightmare. That day customers who got paid on Friday—every week, every two weeks, the first and fifteenth of the month, and the first of every month—came to the bank to cash their checks; that was before the direct deposit, of course. The lines were out the door, and customers were anxiously waiting to get their weekend started. I had mastered the ability to work the drive-in but opted to help those tellers working the regular windows.

"I'll take the next customer with checks only, please." A handsome foreigner came to me and handed me a bunch of checks. I verified the checks and gave him a receipt for his transaction. Whew, finally, four o'clock came around, and we were all tired and ready to go home. I had a wonderful weekend. I felt so accomplished that I had finally found my path. I would be a banker; then it happened. I returned to work the following Monday with a positive attitude and was happy that I was getting good at my job.

"Angela, we would like to see you for a minute," said the assistant bank manager as I started to log out for the day.

"What about?" I asked.

"It seems as if you did a transaction on Friday, and $550 was missing in cash," she informed me.

"What, how can that be? I have the best record on this staff," I said as tears strolled down my eyes.

I had apparently accepted the "checks only" from the business customers, assuming they understood my instructions but did not look at the deposit slip to see if there was cash listed. We called the customer to verify the deposit, but he said he did not speak English. I pleaded with him hysterically, in tears, to tell the truth. "No English," he kept saying. My reaction alone helped them know I did not take the money, but they let me go because I was still on probation. I offered to have the money paid back out of my check, and the assistant manager asked, "Why would you do such a thing?" All I knew was I had made a mistake, and I wanted to make it right, but she was more than happy to make me pay by getting rid of me.

When I saw the smirk on her face, I cried like a baby. I felt so crushed so defeated. I called the only person I knew who would help me get myself together, my grandmother. When I told her, she said, "Baby, you do not have to stay up there. Come on home, and everything will be okay." I got on the bus with silent tears rolling down my face as I left Washington, DC, to Washington, NC. When I got to my grandmother's house, I felt wrapped in a blanket of redemption and comfort. Slowly I regained my composure and found the courage to try again.

I returned home and discovered a medical certificate program at Georgetown School of Science and Arts in which I excelled. Though I earned college credits, part of me was ashamed that it was not the official Georgetown University. Just as I was about to graduate from this program, I went to the school and learned they had filed for bankruptcy, and it was closing. *Another deflating loss,* I thought, but this time there was a silver lining. The school arranged a job fair they'd held for displaced students.

The students had a chance to meet medical professionals right on the spot. I interviewed with an ophthalmologist office and a hospital. I chose to work with the ophthalmologist because they paid me a dollar more. Besides, a former worker and friend told me that she had a horrible work experience at that hospital. As a young teenager, I did not understand benefits, job security, or retirement. All I knew was the money was more, and I wanted to have it. After two weeks on the job, I intuitively knew it was a bad fit; it did not work for me. My mother encouraged me to call the hospital back, and I got a second interview.

I walked into the second interview bright-eyed as ever. Then, I was faced with the dreaded question, "Were you ever fired or asked to leave a job?" Many people who coach you on how to answer those types of questions will frequently advise you to come up with some creative answer, but on this day, all I felt in my heart to do was to tell them the truth and why. Being honest got me that job. I was so glad I did not take the word of my friend's bad experience because that was not my case. For the first time in my life, I felt like I was on the right track. I loved my job. My coworkers were fantastic, and I got a chance to meet some influential people while working there. I was glad for that job, but sometimes people view entry-level employees as unimportant.

It was a Sunday, and the day was moderately busy. Most of the patients in our hospital were regulars, so we built relationships with them. On this day, I was at the admissions desk by myself, and suddenly my day went from an occasional admission to calling the triage team to resuscitate a cardiac arrest. As things began to calm down, suddenly, a cab driver rushed in and told me a patient was having a seizure at the front door. I called the triage team again and spent a few minutes trying to convince the operator this was another code blue. Suddenly, you could hear the triage team running back down the hall. I tried to find a discreet way to tell them some pertinent information and was sternly told, "You've done your job; now let me do mine." The scene haunted me for weeks. I never again wanted to be dismissed as a nonvital member of the team because of my title. Something had to give, so I began exploring my options.

I had always been a fan of a great sitcom. One of our favorite programs was *A Different World*. Watching this show gave me a deep sense that I was missing something out of life, and I began to regret not trying to go to college. I could not believe I had settled for a job instead of following my dreams. I did not know what I wanted to do, but since I did well in the medical field, I thought it would be nice to become a doctor.

My niece, Dominique, had passed away at six months of age from Sudden Infant Death Syndrome (SIDS), and I thought about becoming a pediatrician to take care of children. A co-worker from my part-time clothing job was a former student at Brown University, and she would tell me how she took classes with John F. Kennedy Jr. That made me view college from a totally different perspective. It was more than an education; it was an experience. After work, riding home on the bus, I imagined what my life would have been like if I could have gone to Brown. What would I have done if I met John Jr? I made up my mind and determined I, too, wanted to meet influential people and become an influential person. I did not want to be someone who was looked at as though I had little to offer. I took a leap of faith and began to submit college applications.

I knew I wanted to return to my roots to be closer to my grandparents, so North Carolina was the state I chose to attend school. I took leave from work, and my grandfather and I started visiting colleges. The last, but not least, stop of the tour was the Historically Black College and University, Bennett College, in Greensboro, NC. Everything about Bennett College impressed me. This first all-female school dedicated to educating women of color was rich in social history; the campus was also beautiful. Dr. Maya Angelou was on our board, and Dr. Gloria Scott was our president. Added to their glory was the role Bennett played in letting a little-known Baptist preacher, Reverend Dr. Martin Luther King Jr., speak at their chapel when very few other places gave him a platform. I loved it, but I did think it would be difficult to attend a school without men. That's when I learned about *the path*.

The many gentlemen visiting the beautiful women of Bennett College created the dirt path surrounded by grass. North Carolina Agriculture and Technology was blocks away, and nothing could keep the students from the two schools from socializing. The deciding factor? The gentlemen of Morehouse College, Bennett's brother's school, took a bus trip once a year to visit their beautiful sisters. Presumably, if you attended a school like that, some people would think you attended to find a mate. Perhaps it is an excellent place to find a life partner, but for me, it was a place for me to find my dream.

On my way back to DC, with a spark lit in me so great it could fuel the largest fire, I anxiously waited for my acceptance letter. I tried my best to stay focused at work, and then it happened. I went home and was greeted with, "Congratulations, you have been accepted into Bennett College." I screamed, I laughed, and I shouted for joy. From that point on, work became easy to me because no matter how difficult the days became,

I knew I had a plan—a glorious plan that would take me to limitless place.

The summer was nearly over, and we packed up everything in our Chrysler LeBaron. My mother drove my sister and me to college. I was very happy to be there, but I felt inferior because I did not come from money. There were all kinds of luxury cars there; I was an older student from Southeast Washington, DC, without a legacy of wealth or a powerful name to drop in any conversation. I was just Angie. I was rough around the edges; I felt like I did not fit in, so I had to carve a space for myself by trying to be like some of the people I met at my school.

My mother studied business in college, but she did not graduate with a degree. When she was just a teenage girl, the guidance counselor of her small town told her she was not college material. This elitist determined who she felt could best matriculate in a higher learning environment, a devastating blow to my mother that she never forgot. She was a person from a humble background of parents with little education, but she was smart, strong, witty, and determined. She raised us in the heart of the city when DC was the number one murder capital of the United States. During the era of Mayor Barry's summer job programs, Washington football stars, Georgetown University basketball championships, drug pins' rise and fall, and the birth of Go-Go music, it took a mighty woman to keep her family together with many potential distractions. A lot was going on in the city of Washington, DC. Her determination to succeed caused her to go to bed at night with no food so her children could eat.

Her love was proven time and time again as she worked two jobs just to make ends meet, one of which was at an office building, cleaning bathrooms. She would come home to tell us how the bathrooms were dirty. Some of the most beautiful offices on the highest floors would have unmentionable things left behind for the "help" to clean up. How she maintained her dignity through those days was a testament to her spirit, her strength, and the love she had for children. That is why her heart was broken when she noticed the change in my attitude when I went to college. I had an *air* about me, an air of pride that had no place in the heart of someone whose mother cleaned executive bathrooms just to give her a better life.

For years I was in denial as to why people treated me harshly. I thought that maybe because I had been a female straying away from the stereotypical expectations of a girl from the city, that perhaps within their heart, they held resentment toward me. It wasn't until I began to write this book that I discovered when a person is willing to follow their dreams, there may be lonely nights. I knew I did not come from wealth, but I wanted to change that. My great-grandmother cleaned houses for a Caucasian family, and the $60 I had in my pocket when I first arrived at Bennett was from my last paycheck at work. As a matter of fact, as I watched many people move their things into the dorm rooms with designer luggage, I had many things in trash bags. I was embarrassed to bring those bags out of the car, but somehow, I got them into my dorm room, and I began my journey of matriculating at Bennett College.

Since my classes at Georgetown School of Science and Arts were transferable, and I was twenty years old, I transferred into Willa B. Player Hall, an upperclassman dorm. I can proudly say I stayed there for my entire academic career at Bennett. I quickly made friends, and the ladies on my side of the dorm formed an allegiance called the Soul Sistas. We stuck together. We loved each other, and we were family. In my circle of friends, I met some students from very prominent families—people whose ancestors were significant contributors to society, sat with presidents, and filled the history pages during the Civil Rights Movement. All I could contribute was my sense of humor, my flair for writing, and the glimpse of my dream peeking out whenever I was allowed to shine, but I could not talk about my greatness because standing amid that lineage made me shrink at the thought that I did not belong.

Many nights, I lay in my dorm room longing for affirmation, wishing I had the confidence to be there, but memories of my struggle and lack made me shallow, so I distanced myself even further from the reality of my pain. No one knew it; no one could help me, but I still loved my family deeply. When a person has a scar that makes them feel like they're inferiorly different, it could at some point cause them to have an identity crisis; at least it did for me. While finding my identity, I picked the lane of being wealthy, affluent, accomplished, and elite—light-years from my roots. I placed value on those who had those things and associated shame with myself because I did not. My background was full of love, laughter, and a strong sense of family. For years, I did not know we were poor. I watched my grandmother go out to the garden and pick vegetables for dinner, and we ate the fish my great-grandmother caught and biscuits she lovingly made from scratch. My aunt lived on land that had cows, horses, pigs, and chickens. The time I spent with her was wonderful. At her house, I rode horses, that is, until I fell off, hurt myself, and never got back on one again.

Every night as a child, I slept with my great-grandmother, and as I waited for her to finish reading her Bible and saying her prayers, she would tell me a bedtime story. Sometimes, I had to work for those stories by scratching her head and combing her hair, but nevertheless, the love we shared never made me feel empty or unsafe. It wasn't until I saw a Mercedes and other luxury cars that I began to think material things are the things to value. Years later, one of my friends from an upper-class family told me I should be happy that my family was so close because though her family was big on status, they were small in love. As those words resonated in my heart, they began to tear down the walls of being ashamed of being poor, and I erected a memorial of gratitude for coming from such a rich family. However, I had already solidified my reputation of being "high-minded," of which there was very little redemption.

My first year in Bennett was without direction. I told everyone back home that I wanted to be a doctor, but the subject matter could not maintain my interest. Instead of studying, I partied during the first year. My biology teacher would notice the creativity in my scientific papers and strongly suggested I go to the English Department to major in English. The fact that I got a "D" further validated her point of view, so off I went to the English class. There I met a professor keen enough to stir the embers of my dream.

I was assigned a paper to write about the Greensboro Four. My research paper about that topic led to in-depth discussions about racism from a historical fact and the ramifications of covert racism. My professor loved my work. She told me it was publishable and rewarded me with an "A," thus the beginning of finding my true path. I remember going home for the summer and reading the paper to my grandmother while she fixed dinner for our family. I will never forget her words.

"You wrote that?" she asked with surprise and pride.

"Yes, Ma'am," I said.

"Baby, you are going to do something big with your life."

This woman who could not read, read me that day like a Pulitzer Prize—like I was her pride. Those words have remained etched in my heart forever. My professor sent me to the Communications Department at our school. She thought I would find more fulfillment in an interdisciplinary degree in Broadcast Journalism than I would in being an English teacher, and she was right.

I grew so much with that major that I learned speaking, acting, photography, advertising, marketing, and how to write for TV. Though my overall GPA was low because I did not know what I wanted to do with my life, I excelled in my major once I finally found a home. I recall when I had a paper due, and I wanted to spend time with a very dear friend. He and I would stay up all night talking and playing video games. Everyone was doing their work because it was mid-terms, and our papers were due, but because I started to excel in my major naturally, I did not think I had to develop the discipline of perfecting my craft. My roommate knew I had a paper due, and she scolded me for brushing off my work. I ignored her wise words. What was supposed to be a night of fun ended up being a whole weekend of adventure, good food, hiking in the woods, and dynamic conversation. That took precedence over the work I had to do—that is, until the day the paper was due.

The morning my assignment was due, I ran to the computer lab, sat at the computer, and typed like my fingers had received a Mario boost. As Murphy's Law would have it, everything that could go wrong did. As sweat was falling down my face and my heart was racing, I finally got the printer to work, but I did not have time to read my ten-page paper—not to mention edit it. Once I got a clean copy from the old school printer with propitiated papers, I took the floppy disk out of the computer and used my track skills to run across the campus to turn this paper in with only a few minutes to spare. My paper was now in the hands of fate.

My roommate talked to me about taking my work more seriously, and though I tried to ignore the chastisement, I knew she was correct. About a week later, it was time for us to get our papers back. Low and behold, I got an "A" on the assignment with the comment, "Excellent response to an assignment." My friend was not as fortunate, and she was not very happy at spending all her time working on her paper diligently while I was being irresponsible.

The lesson that should have taught me about diligence created an opposite effect. I became addicted to procrastination. It was as if I got some sick thrill out of living life on the edge of my seat. As time went by and procrastination and its consequences seeped in, I had to realize that slow and steady would get me to my finish line if I diligently stayed on the chosen path.

Roses Have Thorns

"But he that dares not grasp the thorn should never crave the rose." —Anne Brontë

Life at Bennett was outstanding. Things were finally looking up for me. I found my passion, and for once in my life, I felt true happiness radiating in my heart. It was the spring of 1992, and North Carolina A&T was celebrating Aggie Fest. The headline act was the popular Washington DC Go-Go band, Rare Essence. Everyone from the DMV (DC, Maryland, Virginia) was attending to get a slice of the nostalgia of our hometown. My boyfriend and I had broken up, and I was ready to party to get the thought out of my head. Racial tension was high because of the Rodney King beatings in California, so this was a needed distraction.

Dressed to impress, I went to this party, determined to dance the night away. I surveyed the room and suddenly saw a tall, handsome gentleman with a signature style of DC. With one look, I was hooked. I needed his attention, but he did not look my way. I walked over to him and said, "You must be from DC. This is your lucky night; let's go make beautiful music together." The cheesy line made him laugh, and we danced all night. He was a student at Hampton University and a soon-to-be naval officer—the perfect catch, everything I thought a lady could want in a man: smart, funny, and focused.

Our connection was instant. He became my best friend, the man with whom I wanted to spend the rest of my life loving. Our relationship was complicated because, again, the issue of social status came up. For me, all I wanted was him, but some of those who knew him could only see a girl from Southeast DC with little lineage to offer him. What they could not see was the fun we shared. The Rodney King verdict bonded us, as the two of us with so much potential were ready to change the world, but the distance between Greensboro and Hampton, VA, often proved too much to bear.

Summer had come, and I longed to see him more. As our love began to blossom, I wondered if he would ever introduce me to his parents, and then I got the call. "My parents want to meet you," he said. My heart dropped. Nervously, I accepted the invitation and tried my hardest to put my best foot forward. My mother was not happy about how I felt because I walked around the house like I was about to meet royalty, and she wanted me to know *I* was the prize. After several outfits,

I decided to wear a fuchsia pink, pleated skirt and cream blouse with black patent leather heels. I had my hair done in the most beautiful way I could, and I made sure my make-up was flawless. Hand-in-hand we walked into the Sheraton Hotel, and I sat at the table and met his family—full of Ph.D. scholars. What could I possibly tell these people about my background? Would they still like me if I told them we had no money? Would they think I only wanted him for his?

I had all kinds of thoughts going through my head, and finally, I said, "Hello, my name is Angela. Great to meet you." Awkwardly, I sat there for the first minutes after the introduction, and then I felt comfortable being myself. Let my mother tell it, I had always been intelligent, so it was no challenge to speak to them about world issues, politics, religion, education, and the state of the Black community. My answers were sincere and truthful. I stood true to my core, and as a result, they gave me their blessings to date their son.

After dinner, we coasted to my house on the fumes of love. Nothing could bring me down until we got the dreaded call that my grandfather's anemia was not just anemia. It was an issue much more severe, and for the remainder of that summer, the man who protected me, loved me, and provided for me was preparing to make his journey to the afterlife. My friend was a particular comfort for me during that time. He would drive me to North Carolina and support me as only he could, but I felt like I was losing him when my aunt had a cookout and asked us to try her cooking. We both tasted this meat prepared with gravy, onions, and savory spices.

> "Hmmm, this is good," we both said.
> She asked, "Well, do you like bear?"
> "No, Ma'am," I said.
> She replied, "Stop lying; you just ate one."

Unfortunately, she had no choice but to kill a threatening bear on her property. The look on his face *made me think our relationship was over.* I thought we had a good run, but he stayed, and we laughed about it all summer. Things were calm for a bit until July 26, 1992, when my grandfather passed away. I was inconsolable until I realized how fortunate I was to have the man of my dreams. He told me he would be a pallbearer for my grandfather, and I was happy to know my future husband would carry my grandfather to his resting place.

Before my grandfather's passing, he told me he wanted me to marry a man who would love and really take care of me; that was his prayer for me. Stunned at the conversation that had never been breached, I held his prayer close to my heart. My peace was in the fact that my grandfather had seen his prayers answered. There's something beautiful about a woman in love. She opens like a flower. However, as the day of my grandfather's funeral grew near, I noticed the phone calls were few and far between. "Where have you been?" I asked him. He called me to say he would not be able to attend the funeral, and just like that, my love and hope for our relationship were shattered. I accepted his excuse, but the fragments of my broken heart were never the same.

At my grandfather's funeral, everyone in town attended. I looked back at the procession and saw nothing but a sea of cars that seemed not to end. It dawned on me I was the granddaughter of a king, in his own right, and the thought of his not guiding my life was too much for me. I spent the summer of 1992 in a haze. Emotionally, I was in no shape to return to school. My cousin, the late Brian SlickRick Williams, was the lead singer of Hot Cold Sweat Go-Go Band in DC, formerly known as the Crossover Band. I asked him if I could spend the summer with him, working as his marketing manager, and it seemed like a good idea until my boyfriend's mother gave me the money to return to school, for which I would forever be grateful.

The lady I was afraid of meeting because of my humble background believed in me so much that she invested in my future. Her support validated me. It made me feel like I did belong in that circle. I returned to school depressed and still in need of comfort because, though his mother was there for me, her son and I never recovered from what I felt was the ultimate betrayal of my emotions. I tried everything to throw myself into my work, but the nightmares I had of my grandfather's death stalked me every night. I spoke to my Drama teacher about what I was going through, and he talked to me about the Nigerian way of celebrating the life of a person, reveling in the fact that they now joined the ranks of our ancestors. The words he spoke to me about God and the afterlife were a salve to my soul. From that moment, the nightmares left, and I developed a focus like never before to make my grandfather proud.

Shortly after that, I got a job at a grocery store to save money to join Alpha Kappa Alpha Sorority, Inc., with a GPA barely over the minimum requirement. I felt as if I had to prove myself. The sister's GPAs were higher than mine, but not because of my ability; it was because of my lack of focus starting off my academic career. What should have been one of the most exciting times of my life was often overshadowed by my not being able to proudly boast in the glory of a 4.0. I did not realize life was more than a number or a test score; it was the totality of your experiences that brings about a greater value, and I slowly began to embrace that concept.

This understanding got me a job as an editorial assistant for the Greensboro News and Record during my senior year. It was my first experience in the newsroom, and it allowed me to expand my vision. When it was time to graduate from school, I was offered a permanent job at the newspaper. I could not imagine how I could ever live off $4.25 per hour in 1993 with no car and no one to support my cash flow. The opportunity that was presented to me could have been my great break, but I did not have the faith to believe I could make it. The thorn of fear of lack caused me to abandon my dream and move back to the city where I was sure there would be greater chances for me to soar. After all, if a local newspaper wanted me, surely the Washington Post would be knocking my doors down with offers.

I packed up my things and went home to DC to live with my mother. Having earned a bachelor's degree elevated my confidence. I sat out to reach a goal, and I achieved it, but I did not know the road ahead would be different than it was for the sitcom, *A Different World*. I imagined what my life would be like post-graduation; I saw myself getting into advertising and becoming this prominent executive in New York. I kept that dream for most of my time in school until I visited New York and realized that though the city lights were enticing, the noise and the crowd were a bit more than this country girl at heart could tolerate, so I headed back to my beloved DC.

The advertising opportunities were not as plentiful, so I knocked on every door I could until I landed a job at a temporary agency. They sent me to a real estate company in Maryland. Though I had a degree, they offered me a job as a receptionist. With my degree and work background, I could not understand why, but it was a step up from what I was offered in my grandparent's hometown. One summer, while on break, I applied for an office job, wearing a houndstooth suit and my grandmother's pearls. I came in the door with a smile on my face, excited that the employment office had sent me to interview for this job. As soon as I got there, dressed as professionally as possible, the woman looked at me and asked me if I had come to apply for government assistance. I told her no. In fact, I was there to apply for the job. Perhaps it was the humiliation of assuming that I was there for help, or it could have been the tone of my snobby response. Either way, silence gripped the room, and needless to say, they did not offer me the job. If they had, I probably would not have taken it.

The other option the employment center offered me was a job in manual labor at a factory. Though there is absolutely no shame in that, my matriculation was supposed to set me up for more opportunities; at least, I believed that would happen when I applied for student loans. There was one thing I knew for sure, the last time I did anything remotely like that: I was sent home.

The word around town was that they were looking for some hired hands to help pick tobacco, and it was an easy way to make a few bucks. I rode on the back of the truck with those going to the field, excited about the candy I would be able to buy from my day's pay. Picking didn't seem so hard, at least not at first, and then it happened. Sweat pouring down my brow, and with my heart pumping into overdrive, I let out a billowing scream loud enough to wake the dead. Scaring everyone surrounding me, they tried to calm me down to determine if a snake had bitten me. The discovery of a big juicy green tobacco worm presented me with the invitation to go home and not come back.

I loved the outdoors but was not a fan of some of its creatures. Having that past childhood knowledge, I figured that work required a skill set I did not have (humility), but I could be a hostess. So I took a job as a waitress and only lasted one day. I would have worked hard at that job, but the patrons worked me to the bone and gave me only a dollar tip. I could not survive on that, especially since servers make most of their money from tips, so I quit.

My grandmother, though not college-bred, was extremely wise. What she lacked in book smarts, she compensated with common sense and a strong gift of discernment. I was not courageous enough to tell her I quit, but she read my prideful spirit like an open book. I put on my waitress clothes and sat down in the chair before it was time for me to go to work. I figured I'd think of something to tell her as I returned home from spending the entire day at the mall. She was watching *Guiding Light,* a soap opera. For her to be interrupted when "her program" was on, as she so hilariously called it, was to have your concerns fall on closed ears as she would wave her hands at you and say, "Hush a minute," and hush you did. She took her eyes off the screen and stared at me as if she were getting some spiritual download from God, telling her just what I was about to do.

"Ummmhumm," she said, after gazing at me for a bit.

"What?" I asked.

"You look just like you are not going to work today."

Part of me wanted to laugh because that was my "Big Momma," and the other part wanted to run because I knew then there was nothing you could ever tell this woman that she did not already know. God had given her a gift to know, so I might as well have come clean. I kissed her bye and started pretending to go to work. The Carolina heat beamed on my face at such a level that day I could not think of any excuse for returning home. The only thing I could think about was getting out of the heat. I could not continue with this farce. Humbly, I went back to my grandmother and walked through the door. She said, "I knew it," so I told her the truth, and she helped me get a job at the local mall in a department store, and there I found some comfort. I met wonderful customers and enjoyed meeting people of other races. I was good at my job; I had previous retail experience, and my soft skills were always my winning trait.

One of my customers told me how she started from the bottom and had nothing, and God blessed her with everything she could ever want and more—words I never forgot. Recalling those past work experiences helped me swallow my pride. I took the job as a receptionist, even though I had a college degree. I tried to keep a positive attitude. My smile was noticeable to all with whom I engaged. "You're still smiling," a sterned-face employee said to me. "Yes," I agreed. Not long after that, the mean treatment I received and over 300 phone calls a day began to cause me to suffer from anxiety attacks. I could not stand working there, so I declined their permanent job offer and went back to temping.

I got a job assisting a retired general. I worked hard to prove myself as I was happy to have my own office, and then it happened—more racial divide. The OJ Simpson trial made every news medium's front page, and it was time to hear the verdict. Some staff members had small TVs in their offices; we were all on pins and needles when we heard the verdict of "not guilty." The looks on the face of my boss and coworkers were beyond anything I had ever seen; pure disgust is my closest definition. Suddenly, my favor dried up like the Sahara Dessert: no support and no office small talk, only assignments with no direction. I was transcribing notes from a meeting when I got the dreaded phone call.

"Angela, would you see me in my office, please?"
"Yes, sir, right away," I said.

He would not look at me eye-to-eye, but the words he said caught me entirely by surprise.

"We are not going to extend your services with us here. Today is your last day."
"Huh? What did I do?"
"I'm not pleased with the quality of your work.
When you first got here, I thought you were Top Gun," he said, "but that's not the case."

Everything in me held back my urban training to tell him what I really thought about him.

I said, instead, "Sir, when I walked into your door, I was Top Gun, and when I leave out of here, I will still be Top Gun."
"By all means, stay the day and finish your work," he insisted.
I arrogantly replied, "I don't have to wait until the end of the day; I'll leave now."

He signed my timecard, and I gathered my things and did not factor in my bus not leaving for at least three hours. Neither did I have money for a cab. Perhaps, I should have just logged the hours and left with my dignity, instead of staying on the property, waiting for my bus to come looking like a disgruntled ex-employee under surveillance. Where was Spike Lee to coach me through my theatrical departure?

My mother was starting to get worried about me because the anxiety attacks got worse once I got fired, so she suggested I turn to Jesus for help with my anxiety and employment struggles. Every rosy situation I found myself in had many thorns, but as an "educated" person, I did not even want to go to religion. For years, I felt religion had been used to oppress my people as we bowed down to an image of what we thought Jesus looked like, which resembled the race of those with whom we had contention. Though I had grown up in church, I, like many, had fallen away for that very reason.

When I was a child, I saw a beautiful church and asked my grandmother if we could visit it. She told me no because that was the "white" church. Even in my five-year-old mind, I did not understand that concept. Education made me want to explore other spiritual paths, partly because of boredom and life's restrictions in Christianity and partly because of unbelief and my impressions of hypocrisy amongst believers. However, the anxiety attacks got so severe I had to try something. The doctors said it was nothing wrong with me as multiple trips to the hospital and calls to the ambulance were setting me up to go to the mental ward. Though

I had spent my life dealing with many deep-rooted issues related to my burns, I did not think I needed help. Standing in my bedroom, looking up into the sky from my top-floor apartment, I felt strangely close to the God of my elders. "Jesus, if you are real, reveal yourself to me," I prayed. Those words forever changed my life.

Seasons Change

"As long as the earth shall remain, there will be planting and harvest, cold and heat, summer and winter, day and night will never cease.
—Genesis 8:22 (NLT)

As summer gave way to fall, I could see the beautiful leaves beginning to unveil their painted glory. My mother told me I was born for blessings. While she was pregnant with me, she craved concord grapes. She would often tell the story of how she sent my father out in the rain to buy her grapes and how she used to keep them next to the bed, snacking on them throughout the night. My father jokingly told her that I would turn into a grape if she kept it up. I made my appearance into the world at 2:37 a.m.; my mother gave birth to a baby girl with a distinctive birthmark on her arm. "Is that what I think it is?" my dad asked as he examined me. Sure enough, a birthmark resembling a cluster of grapes had memorialized them, reflecting on the night my dad told my mom she was going to give birth to a grape. It was a beautiful reminder of a night of love and laughter, and ultimately a deeper meaning of my purpose.

My mother thought I should be named Fonda Michelle, meaning "Tender, Who is Like God," but my father insisted that I be named Angela, "Messenger of God," because a child with grapes as a birthmark would ultimately have something to tell the world. Regardless of my birthmark symbolism, I did not feel blessed as I looked for jobs and doors remained closed.

The humiliation began to take residence in my mind as people would call me to ask me if I had a job yet. I could imagine them snickering at me as I stood there, a first-generation college graduate with an expensive college degree with no prospect or good fortune coming my way. My aunt Teenie had always encouraged me to keep applying for jobs in various industries. Her persistence in the matter influenced me to apply for a part-time job doing marketing research for a company with excellent career opportunities.

Excitedly, I got the job. In this role, in 1995, I searched newspaper articles worldwide, looking for trends and future innovations that would ultimately challenge the viability of my organization. This job made me more confident, and I felt that things were finally changing for me. I was offered a contract to do this job full-time for at least a year. Finally, I had a position in which I could be proud.

My new apartment and my exciting job made me feel like my life was finally coming together, but I did not have a love interest. The person I had been dating joined the Marine Corp and left me feeling sad and lonely. A friend of mine introduced me to a young aspiring journalist, and our connection was instant. From poetry to intelligent conversations about politics and the state of our culture, I was floating on cloud nine, but not every cloud in the sky brings fair weather. As our relationship developed, I discovered I was going to have our child. Excited to tell him this news, I practiced the words I would say to him in the most poetic manner, sufficient to our artistic connection.

It was at my mother's birthday party that I realized I had made a terrible mistake. He was rude and called my family hillbillies. My uncles were doing a scene from the wrestling shows they watched, and he sat there looking at my family laughing and having fun as if we were so beneath him. He did the very thing I imagine the "elite" would do when they came around. I quietly began to watch him the rest of the night. Everyone was singing when we gathered around to sing "Happy Birthday" to my mother, except him. My heart sank. What had I done? Was this the man I irresponsibly chose to be the father of my child? Would I spend the rest of my life reminded of his ugliness? Would our child have those traits?

I instantly went from happy to incredibly scared. We left the party, and I was at a loss for words. The ride home was quiet, as I realized we would not make it. I said to him, "Do you hear that"? as we rode with only the slight sound of the car. "I don't hear anything," he said sharply. "Exactly," I said. "Exactly." The silence was deep enough to convey a message that no words could ever sufficiently describe. We parted ways and gave each other space to think. After about a week of no communication, I got a call from him.

"How have you been?" he asked.

"I'm okay."

"Not me," he informed me, "I have been sick to my stomach. I think I got some kind of stomach virus."

Bluntly, I said, "I'm pregnant." Those words rendered him speechless.

"Abort it," he demanded. "I don't want to have children."

"I don't believe in abortion," I replied. "It's against my religion."

"Humph, oh really," he stated sarcastically. "What would make you think I would want you to be the mother of my child?"

You could have sold me for a penny because that was how much I felt I was worth—many tears and attempts to get him to see things more positively left me more fragmented. "I'm sick of your shenanigans," he later told me. "If you have this baby, I want nothing to do with you or it."

I decided to walk away and do whatever I could to raise my child without him in the picture. I left him and did not look back, but I was perplexed at how someone could always talk about manhood, racial and cultural progress, and uplifting the community in one breath and be so irresponsible and mean-spirited in the next. I remember him talking about aspirations of running for a political office one day. I could not imagine that ever happening successfully for him, given the truth about who he really was behind the collection of beautiful words he would so eloquently speak and write.

I ultimately confided in my boss and shared what was going on in my life. I thought I was speaking to her confidently. "You need to be careful about telling your business to this boss," her colleague told me. "She has told everyone you are pregnant and alone and that you will probably need to go on welfare." I could not believe my ears. We were all contractors, so I did not know how to handle this information properly, so I did not renew my contract because I was livid. How did I go from finally getting a great job to discovering I worked for a woman who could not be trusted in addition to carrying the baby of a man with such a dark soul?

I somehow found the strength to hold it together and started searching through catalogs to pick out room décor for my child. I was hoping for a little girl that I would name Zoe. I was going into the third month of my pregnancy, and I was excited about hearing my child's heartbeat for the first time. Alone and courageous, I sat waiting for my turn to get an ultrasound. "Just relax," they said. After several tries, they could not locate the baby. I had an anembryonic gestation. In other words, a blighted ovum. This condition is usually discovered at the ultrasound and can take weeks to expel itself from your body. It was Thursday, November 21, 1996, and I had just gotten the devastating news that carrying this pregnancy would end with no baby.

I caught the bus to my mother's house, crying all the way there. I fell on my knees and cried out to God and begged Him not to let me carry that pregnancy anymore. I just did not have the emotional strength to deal with the abuse I suffered from the father and my manager's betrayal at work. The thoughts of carrying around an empty sack, knowing it was all a façade, were catastrophic. Around 8:00 p.m. Saturday, November 22, a sharp pain hit me, and I woke from a deep sleep, screaming and holding my stomach. It went away after a few minutes, and then it came back, each one more intense than the other.

My body was mimicking labor in efforts to expel the pregnancy. My mother had to rush me to the hospital.

We arrived at the Washington Hospital Center, and they took me immediately. When they finally released me from the hospital early the next morning, my mother took me back to her house to recover from the miscarriage. We arrived at 5:30 a.m., and I was physically and mentally exhausted. I crawled into the bed with her and quietly cried myself to sleep while she gave me the most beautiful words of encouragement. "Joy will come in the morning."

She told me I would one day meet someone to love me just like I deserved to be loved. Though it was hard to imagine at the time, I found peace in those words. Since it was Sunday morning, she got up to go to church, and although I was mentally and physically drained, I went with her. We both only had a few hours of sleep, but sitting in the presence of the Lord was the only thing I could think of that would soothe the wounds of my soul. I remember how my mother told me to pray about my anxiety attacks, and when I did, they suddenly went away. If faith could do that for me, what would this Jesus do for my current situation?

Slowly I walked into the church with my mother and my eyes full of tears. The late Reverend Henry Harper was the pastor of St. Mark African Methodist Episcopalian Church and a native Carolinian. He stood in the pulpit as a beacon of light from a lighthouse guiding me in from my storm, beckoning, "Perhaps there is someone out there who needs prayer; the altar is open for you." Even though my knees were feeble, I went up there, then knelt and talked to God. I did not know Him and had no real connection of my own. I just knew when I prayed for healing from anxiety, it went away, and that's when I began associating with Christianity. Still, I did not pursue a deeper relationship with Him until that day at the altar. I just wanted the pain to stop. Though I had grown up in church, my spiritual connection was superficial. It was time for me to reconnect authentically. Growing up, my great-grandmother had a circle of missionary friends who would often visit and call our home. There was one lady in her group who came across as very mean. When she called my great-grandmother, she would say curtly, "Is Ida there?" I would ask, "May I ask who's calling, please?" Then, she would say, "None of your business." I certainly did not want to be like her.

In school, I got in a debate in one of my literature classes about the Bible, as I mentioned the beauty of its poetry. One of the young ladies argued with me and told me how she would not allow me to sit there and talk about the Bible in that way. I looked at her and asked, "What do you mean? The Bible is full of poetry." Though I had a superficial relationship with religion and had no desire to live a strict lifestyle, I still remembered the days I read the Bible as a teenager. Our debate got so intense that the professor had to intervene, but not before I told her, "That's why no one wants to go to church—because of people like you." I knew I did not want to be like her, either.

The extremes between living a life of bitterness and an inaccurate understanding of the scriptures were disincentives for me; however, I was compelled to give my spirit a chance to connect with my life source. I went up to the wooden altar and kneeled to pray, and all I can remember was crying until I emptied a puddle of tears into the grooves of the altar. When I got up, I felt a tremendous load had been lifted. I had a new purpose, a new direction. "If any man is in Christ Jesus, old things are passed away," I was told. "Behold, all things are new."

It was as if I was a brand-new baby. I wanted to tell the world about Jesus—to let everyone I encountered know about the love of a man that saved me from myself. I was headed for self-destruction, but God saved me! The low self-esteem I had all my life due to the third-degree burns and how people used to call me horrible names because of my scars left me dysfunctional. I knew I needed some help in changing my life, and perhaps religion would provide me with the tools to do so.

With my newfound faith, I discovered Bishop T. D. Jakes's book, *Woman Thou Art Loosed*. I would read it during my spare time. As fate would have it, the temporary agency I had previously used had another job at the company I had just left, but it was a secretarial position this time. Because I had no income and was learning humility, I decided to take the job. I began working in their operations department. At the time, I was assigned next to a lady who was an expert at Microsoft Office. I knew little about the Office programs; I barely passed the test to get the job, but she was willing to train me, for which I will always be eternally grateful. She talked to me about my clothes and how to do presentations like a pro. I admired her. My dewy-eyed view of life and my responses to it prompted her to tell me that I looked at life through rose-colored glasses, and it's just not that way.

When I got up off my knees at the altar after having a miscarriage, I did not leave the altar; I relocated it to my heart. I then began to want to help people, spread love, smile, and tell people about my experience in hopes that they could one day enjoy the light that had entered my heart. I was in for a rude awakening. Not long after going to church and doing well, I was introduced to a *supposed* minster who tried to convince me that the things I would do one day would require me to come out of the church and ostracize my family because they just were not able to go with me where I was going. I was like a baby lamb, willing to follow the wolf anywhere it led me if he told me I could find Jesus there. Sharing this information with a wonderful first lady in my office helped me finally get to a place where I could see the lies being told to me, but not without the consequences of breaking relationships that had meant the world to me. Heeding this "spiritual guru's" advice caused me to leave the safety of my church and turn my back on my family, a decision I regret to this day.

I disappointed a lot of people, thinking I was following my spiritual path. The gentlemen I had been seeing had proposed to me, but I was not in a fully healed condition to accept it. It seemed like the track of new enlightenment was filled with deception and opportunism. I was too blind to see it. I needed a change, so I decided to cut the relaxer out of my hair and loc my natural mane to celebrate my spiritual journey. When the hairdresser turned me around, I saw myself in the mirror in my natural state and cried. What had I done? I saw the images fed to me all my life growing up of mammies and sambos. I did not see a wonderfully and fearfully made woman with a hair of wool, so I opted to wear hats.

While on a date, I tried to hide my scar and my hair, and my date said to me, "How come people always try to hide what's unique about them?" He validated me, and that one act of kindness gave me the courage to take my hat off and stop hiding my burns. I went out and accessorized to accentuate my new look. Ashamed of how God had made me, I needed a boost to my ego. I went to work, and many people put their heads down when they saw my tiny little twisted hairstyle. In the nineties, loc'd hair was a fashion faux pas. Though

Bob Marley was an icon who transcended races, most people disapproved of his hairstyle, particularly with women and especially in Corporate America. I went into my boss's office to give her a phone message, and she was so engrossed at laughing in her conversation that she did not hear me coming nor see me standing at the door. I stood there long enough to hear, "Did you see her hair?"

Suddenly the inflation of my self-esteem balloon was popped by the words of an insensitive manager. When she saw me, she turned pale as a ghost. She tried to keep her composure, but our relationship became very awkward after that. "I would sue," someone told me, but I knew it was her words against mine, so I opted not to sue, especially since I was a temporary employee. I requested a transfer, and they found me another assignment working in the finance department.

What an opportunity I had in this department. The staff was wonderful, and my manager was one of the coolest bosses I had ever had. He and I were cut from the same cloth. The only issue we had was his manager. She was tough and often difficult to please, but we figured it out together. In this department, I was encouraged by religious folk to cut my hair because it would block me from being blessed. I did not understand how God could make us with such versatile hair and then ask us to change its texture to be deemed beautiful or, even more, found worthy of work. Nevertheless, I cut my locs and wore what my friends called a "TWA" or teeny weenie afro. My boss never made me feel bad about my hair; he gave me the nickname "Curly Top," and all was well with me for a while.

By now, I had developed quite a reputation for myself. The way my manager treated me gave me the confidence I needed to focus on developing my administrative skills. Instead of building walls, I built a brand. I became known for my soft skills. I decided to build a relationship with everyone who crossed my path. Whenever we would have a catered meeting, I always saved plates for the maintenance crew. I called people on holidays and even went to their cubicles just to see how they were doing. That became my strategy for success: connection, gratitude, follow-up, and consistency. Eventually, my reputation for having outstanding interpersonal skills began to precede me. As a result, I became a temp who was in high demand.

Under the suggestion of some managers and friends, I reluctantly took the company's secretarial test. Though I had no desire to be a secretary, it was my foot in the door. A friend of mine told me about a staff assistant position that had recently become available, and I applied for it. When I met the manager, I instantly knew that we would be a great fit. He was a super smart Harvard graduate with a love of the Tour de France and a heart of gold. Before the interview was over, I was hired. We spent most of the time talking about the job, but I was most impressed by his brilliance. This man knew something about everything. Most of our conversations ended with me laughing because I had never met an individual with high intelligence and a humble heart. It was the combination that was so intriguing.

Though I was a secretary, I worked for him with a spirit of excellence. As a result, I only remained his secretary for one month and was quickly asked to sit in the seat of the senior secretary, as our department head had just gotten promoted to vice president. I could not believe my good fortune. I accepted the detailed position, but not before I was given an unsolicited nugget that left me in awe. The secretary told me to be careful about how I treated people on my way up. He said to me, "The vice president job our director was about to take would be over a person she used to work for who mistreated her." I knew the manager she used to work for, and she was not a gentle person.

I could not believe how that situation had turned. I did not know the dynamics of the relationship between both parties, but I do know the mean boss retired soon after. Throughout my career, I took that lesson with me and applied the golden rule of treating people like I wanted to be treated to my career toolkit. From that moment on, I was in for the ride of my life. I had gone from a contractor to a career employee. I had finally found an organization I could call home. All the cold days and lonely nights were finally changing to blossoms of promise; the best was yet to come.

The new director of our department was a shrewd businesswoman. There was not one thing going on in her department of which she was unaware. If a person tried to come in late, she knew it. Whatever the scenario, she was on top of it. For every problem, this woman had a solution. Her former employee told me she had worked her way up from a secretary and that I could learn a lot from this lady just by assisting her. I studied her ways and gleaned from her the lesson of organization.

She was demanding but not degrading. She never asked you to do things she had not done or was unwilling to do. She was an equal opportunity stickler. She did not care about your race, gender, or any other factor. Her standards were her standards, and I learned to respect her tremendously because of it. Sometimes, I felt inadequate working with her because she was so organized, and I was an artsy type with no real system on how to do things. Keeping up with her was a challenge. "Angela, I need to talk to you, she said." I thought she was going to update me on the role I would play in preparing for our reorganization. I did not expect to hear the words that would shape my destiny.

> "I've decided to hire the person sitting next to you because she and I have worked together before, and I believe it will be a greater fit."

"What about me?" I inquired. "The job I had before has been eliminated; I have nowhere to go. Am I fired?"

"No," she assured me, "you will both trade places." Tears welled up in my eyes; I could not help but think I was not good enough for the job.

"This job is for someone interested in advancing their administrative assistance abilities. The other job is good for someone who wants to get into staff work."

Now, my first thought about this was anger. I must admit I did not see anything great; I saw it as a stab in my back, and to be honest, I defaulted to a victim mentality. After getting over the initial shock, I switched seats with the secretary next to me the following Monday. Though we were still side-by-side, she—in her already-permanent job—requested a noncompetitive transfer into the job I was working in, and I did not appreciate it one bit. Once again, I had to prove myself in this detail and even compete with other applicants to get the job permanently. If the saying about your attitude determining your altitude was true, I knew I was in trouble. *Here we go again,* I thought.

Obstacles, Offenses, and Opportunities

"Opportunity often comes disguised in the form of misfortune or temporary defeat." —Napoleon Hill

I spent the entire weekend talking to people about the "switch." I was hurt and angry and did not know how to go to work and pretend I wanted to be there, but I went anyway. I went into the new manager's office with the mindset that the organization was no longer a good fit for me, and it was just a matter of time before I left. I resented the conversation that led to the switch. It shook my world. I had only been a permanent employee for a year, and now I found myself having to compete for my job. I could not see the forest for the trees. "Oh, woe is me, Lord!"

My new manager was a wonderful woman of God from Minnesota. Our department disseminated information and created policies, procedures, and programs. We also brought all the area offices together to ensure one voice from headquarters throughout the country. We had a significant job, but not one I was interested in doing. From the first weeks, I displayed my negative attitude by rarely smiling and barely talking. My work performance was not good, and I began to make many mistakes. My manager and I would get into disagreements, and I started to overuse my sick leave. The thought of going to work while watching the secretary next to me smile and enjoy the staff I had built a relationship with was more than I could handle. It never dawned on me that I was still "auditioning" for this job.

The lack of professionalism I began to show started to break any possible relationship I could have with my manager, and rightfully so. I felt as if she was in on the "scheme" to get rid of me, and I did not care how amazing I used to think she was. At that point, she, too, had become my enemy. I would go home and tell my mom how horribly we were getting along and how I wanted to leave, and she advised me not to do it. I became increasingly despondent because I felt no one was listening to how miserable I was at work. Taking matters into my own hands, I started interviewing with other companies with the thought process of leaving, even if I had to go back to temping. I wanted to quit, and to my surprise, I was about to get fired.

My manager called me into her office, and I went in there with the biggest chip on my shoulders I could find. This woman, beautifully and wisely, created a safe environment for us to talk about our problems. I told her I felt like I had no other option but to take this job I did not want. "You always have options," she said to me sternly. "Never forget that. You could either choose to stay or leave, but you will not stay like this." Thinking I was so much smarter than I was, I said hurtfully, "I can come in here and do my work, and unless it pertains to work, I will not talk to you, and you don't have to talk to me," as I put my head down. What came next was the most loving response. "Now, that will not benefit either of us, would it?" she inquired.

Suddenly, out of the blue, we both started laughing. I sat in her office and laughed until I cried and apologized to her for my reaction to the change. This woman was a master coach. She helped me understand the stages of change and lovingly included me in the big functional picture. I felt she heard my voice. For the first time in my career, I felt important and replaced the frown on my face with a smile resonating from a relieved soul.

The turnaround in our relationship became obvious in our office. Our mutual respect developed to such a point that she became my mentor. On one occasion, she brought me back a gift she picked up during her travels. I was grateful just to be at a place where I missed her and wanted her to hurry back from her vacation, but to have her think enough of me to bring me back a trinket took my heart over the moon. I opened her little gift bag, and there it was—a beautiful ceramic oyster with a pearl in it.

"Thank you so much!" I exclaimed.

"Do you know the story of the oyster and how it creates a pearl?" she asked.

"No, I don't."

She explained to me how the oyster gets sand in its shell, and it causes such an irritation that it produces a strong material called nacre to protect itself. She used that moment to enlighten me about the struggles I had gone through in my life. Though she was talking about work, I could not help but think about all the pain and heartache I had experienced.

Looking back at that time, I recall how that advice shaped my mindset about work. This paradigm shift gave me the ability to overcome my obstacles with greater focus. Up until that point, I viewed everything that happened to me in my life as some sort of dark cloud following me. *No one person should suffer as I did,* I often thought. As I got older, I started to heed the words of my dear mother, who told me, "In any given situation, we are not the first ones, the only ones, or the last ones to go through the same situation." Knowing I would face challenges in my life due to the inward scar my outward scar left me, my mother never gave me the luxury of feeling sorry for myself, nor did she tolerate my pity parties. This stern approach to dealing with me often made me feel unsupported, but no one on this earth ever supported me like my mother after my grandparents died.

Children rarely have the mental capacity to understand the wisdom in their parents' words. It is not until the child grows and becomes a parent that those words come full circle. I began to realize every time I was hurt; she was hurt. She felt my pain. Although my miscarriage robbed me of the ability to relate fully, I acknowledge that motherhood can allow you to feel deeply for your child and your desire is not for them to suffer but to do well.

The obstacles in my life were creating irritants, but unlike the oyster, I was not producing the right material to protect myself. A negative mindset kept me bound. It created more negativity in my world. I had to adjust. I began to focus on my work, and as my mentor would talk to me about my mistakes, I still had a hard time receiving feedback because I had spent my entire life listening to people criticize me.

I've heard:

- "You're not pretty enough."
- "You're not skinny enough."
- "You're too dark."
- "Your hair is not long enough."

- "You did not come from wealth."
- "You're not smart enough."
- "You're not good enough."

Those limiting words had begun to take residence in my subconscious mind. Anyone that said anything remotely fitting into one of those categories triggered a reaction and not a response. My reaction to her constructive feedback *was she never sees the good I do*, but my response should have been: are there any classes I can take to get better?

Working in policy requires accuracy. Using the wrong words or omitting a word could cost the organization money for lack of compliance or even lawsuits. She was teaching me how to be thorough, but there was still work to be done because I was very immature. My spiritual growth started to shape my work ethic. I had to learn the lesson of Proverbs 22:29 (NLT). "Do you see any truly competent workers? They will serve kings rather than working for ordinary people."

I took this spiritual principle and began applying it to my work. During my mid-year review, we set developmental goals for me. I had made an embarrassing mistake while planning a meeting where we hosted leaders from around the country. Unfortunately, I had forgotten to provide their names to security for access to the building. This was humiliating to my manager and frustrating to the participants who had spent their time traveling and tugging luggage around the airport.

I knew I was in trouble because there was no way out of this mistake. I did not want to face the managers I inconvenienced or the manager I inadvertently humiliated because of my negligence. These meetings were a part of my manager's corporate goals with her boss. My failure was her failure. Thankfully, the managers were gracious, but the late food arrival for the all-day meeting was yet another strike. I was convinced that was the end of my career. After the meeting, she called me in for a debrief and had me rate myself.

> "How do you think it went?"
> "Terrible," I said.

Nodding her head, I could only imagine what would come next. I've heard people say, "Never let them see you sweat," but I was sweating. I humbly apologized, and she let me know it could not happen again. She used my mistake as a teachable moment. "When you are in charge of a project or event, everything that goes wrong is a reflection of your lack of preparation," she said. I wanted to cry. Those defeating words were seeping back up in me again. *I'm into art, not this. How can I ever feel comfortable doing this job?* I thought. As I faded in and out between the words she said to me and the conversation I was having in my head, I heard her say, "Training." Something in me perked up.

> "I would like to do that," I shared. "Would you be willing to pay for me to take some classes?"
>
> "Yes," we will take it one class at a time."

I researched event production and was approved to take classes at the George Washington University Event Management program. I could not have been more thrilled. I learned and applied, learned, and applied, understood and applied; this was my winning combination. I developed a checklist of best practices and a list of things that went wrong. We grew from being humiliated to being honored for our events. We both were happy with the feedback about our events.

We were a textbook example of the forming of a team. We formed under the most unlikely circumstances. We weathered the storms of conflict and the rocky beginnings of misunderstandings and offenses. With time, dignity, respect, set expectations, and accountability, we began to normalize how we did things. That normalization created a fail-proof system, which allowed us to streamline our processes and optimize our performance. My work was at such a level that I began getting monetary awards for my outstanding work. Suddenly, my name became synonymous with getting results. The Nationwide Conference for Executives was a big deal in the organization. It was a time for all executives to gather to receive the vision for the coming year as well as motivation, leadership, and coaching. Gleaming from the newfound synergy of our team, I could not have anticipated the phone call that changed the course of my career.

"Hello, this is Angela. May I help you?"

"Yes, Angela, this is the Executive Conference Committee, and we want to discuss an opportunity with you."

"Sure," I enthusiastically responded.

"We would like to invite you to work on the committee for our upcoming conference. Your name has come highly recommend."

Say something; say something, I thought to myself. "Oh, that's wonderful," I said. "I would be honored to do so. What does it entail?"

They told me that I would be away from the office at a hotel for a few days, serving the conference team. *The opportunity of a lifetime,* I thought. I knew I had to get permission to join the team. Would my manager agree to let me go? I knew we had our differences over the past two years, and all I could do was hope my past actions and attitude would not hinder me from progressing. Perhaps I had redeemed myself.

When I told my manager about the request for my services, she was happy to give me her support. The lesson she taught me about leadership that day was the power of redeeming your workers. Some leaders write their employees off as useless when they make errors. They never let the person recover from a mistake and hold it against them throughout their entire career. I was surprised that she was happy for me. She earned my love, respect, and loyalty. I had positive energy for the rest of the day. I could not stop smiling, and it was not easy to concentrate on my work. I think I stepped away from my desk more often than usual because I just could not contain my praise or my happiness. It was hard to comprehend what had just happened to me, and I wanted to soak it all in without appearing too excited.

Life had handed me a beautiful lesson on humility. Up until that point, I thought I was a humble person. I once recall seeing a custodian get on her knees to scrub an egg off the floor from a juvenile egg fight and did not like how it made me feel. Though I did not participate in the food fight, I envisioned the messes my mother cleaned up in the executive bathroom suites, my grandmother cleaning laundry at the local hospital, and even thoughts of my great-grandmother working as a maid. At that time, I made up my mind that I did not want to live my life treating the custodian differently from the executive. I felt that decision made me humbler than most. What I did not realize is that pride is just like an onion. Once you get past one layer, there is another right behind it.

Working at the conference made me think about my dreams of working in New York City in advertising. Though the scale was smaller, events had all the things I needed in my life—lights, cameras, and action. It was oxygen to me. I entered an atmosphere where I could clearly see the road ahead of me. I met so many wonderful managers from across the nation, and customer service was easy because I loved what I was doing. I could barely sleep at night and gladly got up early to serve with my team. My smile was contagious. The warmth and happiness that showed in my expression reflected my gratitude.

If you ever have walked in shoes that hurt your feet, you know exactly how it feels to take them off and replace them with a shoe that fits. Finding your passion unlocks the doors to your destiny. From the moment a child goes to school, the objective seems to be to prepare them to survive and not thrive. Survival is good, and it is, of course, essential, but tapping into the discovery zone of what fuels your soul is greater than gold. Throughout our organization, I saw people angry, disgruntled and disengaged in their work. They only did enough to get by, and going beyond that was unfathomable. Many people in support roles were unpleasant and unapproachable, and I could not understand why. Rarely did they smile, and often they looked at me as if I were some flunky, but I realized a secret to success was to first get past the pride of "That's not my job." I knew I had the potential to do much more than typing letters. Taking advantage of assignments without monetary compensation ultimately prepared me for opportunities that would pay me.

After returning from working at the Executive Conference, I had a new attitude. I picked up a part-time job in a nearby clothing store and began to build my wardrobe again. I had to look the part. I set my intention on making all my internal and external customers feel special. Small talk was my way of getting to know them. Whenever we reengaged, I made it a point to build on our previous conversation. "Last time I spoke to you" would be the way I started my conversation. I learned to make humor a part of my brand, and I waited patiently for my change to come.

Our reputation for putting on dynamic meetings earned us the privilege of producing all the functional events in our department. Our new acting vice president was the son of one of the Tuskegee Airmen. During our Black History Program, I was asked to produce the event with them being the main attraction. I no longer had the strength of the Executive Conference Team to help me shine; I had to coordinate this event by myself. I must admit; I was intimidated because this was not a small meeting of familiar participants. This was opened to internal and external guests in the building. To make a mistake at this level would be a career-limiting move.

I talked to my manager about my concerns, and she coached me through the entire process. Collectively, we put together a memorable event—one of which people talked about for weeks. The classes I took at GWU were helping me develop. One of the beautiful things about the event program was the external event training opportunities throughout the city. I was committed to learning all I could about this new career path, so I did not mind investing my time and resources outside my regular work hours. Reaching my full potential was the goal. Proverbs 18:16 (NKJV) states, "A man's gifts makes room for him and brings him before great men." I had no idea a shift in my thinking would be the catalyst for this scripture to come to pass.

After class one night, I learned about an opportunity to volunteer at a high-profile dinner. I wasn't familiar with the event, but I was asked to work in the VIP room. That night, I served Michael Steele, Kathleen Matthews, and Hillary Clinton and was asked to escort the late senator John McCain to his seat. When I shook Mr. McCain's hand, I was moved by how gentle he was. He was humble and pleasant and made me feel appreciated for showing him to his seat. It was indeed the proudest moment in my career.

The event was held at a hotel in Washington, DC, and the event staff booked the presidential suite to be our command office. After the event, I went up to the hotel, stood on the rooftop, and looked at the American flag blowing in the wind. *How did I get here?* I thought about my grandmother and began to get emotional. Since I was not alone on the roof, I held it together best I could, but I knew had she lived to hear me tell her about that, she would have been incredibly proud of me.

I knew I had to leave the event soon since I had to work the next day. I did not want to be late for my "real" job. I gathered my composure and my things and headed for the subway. Dressed in my best suit, I waited for the train to come. It was getting late, and I was ready to get home. Finally, my train arrived. I saw a man in the distance who looked vaguely familiar. As we both got on the same train, his presence came into my focus. It was my ex, the would-be father of my child. Instantly, my blood started boiling. He acted as if he did not know me. I struggled with whether I should tell him that I had a miscarriage. I thought about my powerful night and decided to extend him grace—to free his conscience and forgive him for all he had said and done to me.

I walked over to him and said, "Hi, how have you been? Would you like to know what happened?" Sharply he looked at me as if I were invading his space. His response to me left me somewhat shaken.

"About what?" he asked me with an ominous tone.

I stood there looking straight through to his soul and determined he was not worth the instant vile I had flowing through my veins. I refused to say another word and immediately got off that train and went to the next one behind it. I brushed the dust off my feet and took my peace with me. Upset about what had just happened to me, I reminded myself of what God had just done for me, and I was not going to allow the devil to steal my joy. It took me a minute to get myself together from that encounter, but the words my mother spoke to me never rang truer. "The day will come when you will be glad you did not have his child." Though I would have loved my child if the Lord had seen fit for me to have the baby, I found peace in knowing I never had to deal with him again. He was a mirror of my bad choices, and his indifference helped me understand the importance of the closed door.

For years, I belabored the closed door. Whenever a relationship would break, I wasted days, weeks, months, and sometimes years trying to force my will on the will of God for my life. His will is a perfect will, and His *no* is not meant to reject us but rather redirect us to something better. On that day, I experienced sunshine and rain at the same time. I cried on the rooftop of the hotel because I had seen a glimpse of the glory of God in my life. I wept at home after the encounter with my ex because I got a glimpse of the girl I was before Christ. Understanding why I ran into that man on the same night I experienced my career breakthrough may always remain a mystery to me. However, what I do know is my experience that night made me realize I wanted to wait on the Lord of my salvation for my divine mate.

My life was finally beginning to align with my vision of doing great things. I was ready for my next journey. Through prayer and fellowship, the eyes of my heart were enlightened. I began to think I had more to offer the world than a high-powered career. It was my time to serve the Lord, and I began to do so in a dynamic way. I joined a prison ministry and served at a women's correctional center. There I met some of the most resilient women I have ever known.

These were women who, for some reason, lost sight of who they were or perhaps never had it in the first place. God met them right there. We ate with them, talked with them, encouraged them, and provided workshops to connect or reconnect them to Christ. The God of the universe had touched the women society had thrown away. Lovingly, I watched the Lord minister to their brokenness caused by years of pain of guilt and condemnation. Many of those ladies had a hard time facing the fact that life had handed them such an experience at the perceived hand of God. It was not until the Lord helped us understand there are things out of our control, but there are other things we can control. We may struggle with forgiving God and the people who created our issues for the things that happen to us out of our control. For the things in our control, we struggle with forgiving ourselves. Both situations can leave a root of bitterness in us, and as bitterness takes place in our hearts, every fruit from the tree of our life will be difficult to swallow.

We read about healing nations and having good fruit in the scriptures, but a tree cannot bear healthy leaves or fruit if the root is diseased. When I served those ladies and understood the pain they experienced, I thought about the bitter roots I had in me due to things out of my control. While I was bringing healing to them, it dawned on me that perhaps this physician needed to heal herself. The process of healing can be extremely painful. It was excruciating for me to humble myself to my boss, but the rewards exceeded my expectation. Serving in the prison ministry was challenging and emotional, but I learned the posture of gratitude. Those women were thankful for us coming to see them as some of their parents and families had deserted them. The emotional suffering they experienced at never getting any mail or even an "I love you" was like pouring salt on an open wound during every mail call. I recall us bringing colorful napkins with balloon art on them to celebrate their new commitment to Christ. Our sisters on that journey were thankful; some even broke down and cried. I could not believe what I was seeing.

The week before serving at the prison, I served on the conference team at a megachurch, and the women who came up to us complained about everything from standing in line to the items in the conference gift bags. I even saw pastors act as if they were way too important to speak, and their assistants would cut the line in front of people requesting service by name-dropping an important VIP. I could not help but think of the scriptures that said the least shall be the greatest in the kingdom of God. "But many who are the greatest now will be least important then, and those who seem least important now will be the greatest then" (Matt. 19:30, NLT)

Volunteering my time at the prison created a tremendous shift in my understanding of freedom, appreciation, and choices. The things I had desired in my life were in line with the things I had learned about prosperity: fancy car, high-paying job, money, trips, the "good" life. Chasing those things alone gave me a distorted view of my purpose. Once again, the Lord was working on my heart—line upon line, precept upon precept, here a little, there a little.

I decided to stop feeling ungrateful for my humble beginning and to start enjoying my journey. This approach to work was the key to getting out of the secretarial field. It was nearing the end of the fiscal year, and we needed to give out service and recognition awards in our annual town hall meeting. This event was big because our organization within the company had reached and exceeded many milestones. One of the goals I had in my improvement plan was to attend Toastmasters International. In that professional affiliation, I met inspirational speakers and booked one who used comedy in his presentation about overcoming disabilities. He was a perfect fit for our meeting. We received funding to have him as our speaker, and the rest was history.

I chose the most professional, cost-effective caterer. The employees entered a room transformed into a place of beauty, class, and appreciation. The meal was buffet-style, and the centerpieces to the table were small desserts on a glass tier. The event appeared to look expensive, but the caterer already had that inventory and gave it to us at minimum cost. While everyone was seated, I directed the event.

All the managers in our organization had a chance to see me at work. I could hear people talking about how the room was beautiful and classy. I had soft music playing in the background as they began to eat, and eventually, I was finally able to take my seat as well. Our guest speaker started his inspirational keynote speech. The staff had no clue about what they were going to hear. He walked up to the stage, obviously different from those who sat. He took the mic and wowed the audience from beginning to end. I looked around the room, and people were in tears—not because of his disability but because of laughter. At that moment, all the hard days we had before that event had seemed to go away. Laughter healed us, and my career went from stalled to meteoric.

Rising Star

"Oh, the places you will go." —Dr. Seuss

It seemingly was a routine workday at our company. My manager and I were getting along great. Our days were filled with laughter and good intention. I learned to appreciate her sternness. She was a no-nonsense, no excuse, do-it-right-the-first-time type of boss, but she was fair. We often sat in the office and reflected on our start, and quickly our conversation would go to praising God. Having a godly manager was a gift from the Father, disguised as a thorn in my flesh.

The assumption I had about working for a Christian was a Bible-quoting, song singing, pie-in-the-sky type of expectation. It was furthest from the truth. She taught me to understand the value of stewardship. She helped me understand that we don't work for ourselves but unto the Lord. We work, not so we can get accolades, though those recognitions are outward rewards for a well-done job, but for His glory. This principle helped shape my brand.

While waiting for my big break, I developed contentment with my job. Over the years, I encountered people who had become complacent or perhaps comfortable with their paychecks, unwilling to try and do better, partly because of past rejections and partly due to fear of the unknown. I knew I did not want that for myself. Patience was having a perfect work in me as written in James 1:2–4 (KJV), "My brethren, count it all joy when ye fall into divers temptations; knowing this, that the trying of your faith worketh patience. But let patience have her perfect work that ye may be perfect and entire, wanting nothing."

I honestly did get to a place at my job where I wanted for nothing. My attendance was excellent, I got to work on time, and my wardrobe was good. My service to God was fulfilling. I had financial difficulties and some personal relationship challenges, but overall, I was happy because I believed brighter days were coming my way. At last, it came. It was a beautiful fall day in November when I got the phone call.

> "Hello, may I speak to Angela, please?" the caller asked.
>
> "This is she," I responded curiously.
>
> "Angela, Can you step away for a minute?"
>
> "Sure."

I stepped away to the place where I had coordinated the successful town hall meeting and walked into one of the conference booths. I called the manager right back and stood in awe when she asked me to consider taking a detail at her conference center. I flashed back to a meeting I had there and recalled telling the Lord I wanted to work at the center and live in that city one day. I had driven through a street filled with mansions to get to the building. It was a wonderful property. Butterflies, bees, hummingbirds, birds, and deer were just some of the attractions. The mature trees put on a show every spring and fall. I quickly told her I would be honored to take the assignment, pending my manager's approval. It came with a raise, an office of my own, and developmental opportunities to permanently get me out of the secretarial field.

The moment I stopped being anxious about my career and found peace in my current place was when I was positioned for greater things. Most of the anxiety I experienced had everything to do with how I needed something to tell people about my success. I was overwhelmed with others' opinions, and just when I thought the pride was gone, deep in my heart was a layer of *I can't wait to tell people what I'm doing now.* The first thing on my personal agenda was to get a business card with my title. Somehow, seeing my name on that card was somewhat equivalent to seeing my name in lights. It meant I was succeeding at my goals. Until that point,

I felt like my ascension was slow, at least compared to others, but now I understand slow is not always bad. There are times when fast is appropriate, but discerning those times is not an easy task.

Years ago, a senior citizen I knew died on the highway from driving too slowly, and there are times when I have seen people racing through residential areas driving entirely too fast. Both speeds are dangerous when executed at the wrong time. From the moment we are born, we are taught the importance of time—time to wake up, time to sleep, time to eat, time to leave, and so forth. Therefore, our perception can center around a timetable that we or someone else creates for ourselves.

Working in the prison ministry taught me something about time I never knew. There is a chronological or sequential time (i.e., years, months, days, hours, minutes, and seconds). An example is the celebration of a birthday or anniversary, holiday, etc. I used chronological to determine where I should be in life. By the time I was a certain age, I felt I should have accomplished everything on my list. When it did not happen in those sequences, I became frustrated waiting.

When I let go of my frustrations and began to embrace the journey, the *Kairos* time was revealed to me. The Kairos time is God's set time, a special time not dictated by a clock. It is an opportune time, a time of favor. Psalm 102:13 (KJV) states, "Thou shalt arise and have mercy upon Zion: for the time to favour her, yea, the set time, is come." That was what I was experiencing—God's set time. All the hard work I had done had put me on the radar and opened doors, but I seemingly fell flat when I tried to move outside the rhythm of His set time. In retrospect, had I listened to my elders, perhaps I could have arrived at my Kairos sooner, but I thought I knew everything so foolishly I did it my way.

Sometimes when I speak to young people, I realize wisdom is missing in their lives. In our human experiences, we are all given two choices for learning. We could learn the easy way by gleaning from the lessons of those who have gone before us and applying them to our lives, or we can learn the hard way, ignore sound counsel, and let experience be our teacher. In time, I have come to understand that experience is a taskmaster. When I think about Jesus, the Son of the living God, I think about how He sat with the elders of the land and learned from them. He humbled himself enough to allow them to develop Him. Though part man and part God, the man in Him knew enough to respect those who had gone before Him. Luke 2:41–47 teaches us after Mary and Joseph went to Jerusalem for the Passover Feast when Jesus was twelve years old, Jesus remained behind after the festivities, but His parents supposed Him to be in the caravan and traveled a day's journey. When they *began* searching for Him, they went back to Jerusalem. "*Three days later, they found Him in the [court of the] temple, sitting among the teachers, both listening to them and asking them questions. All who heard Him were amazed by His intelligence and His understanding and His answers" (Luke 2:46–47, AMP).*

I had finally settled down enough to heed the wisdom of my mother and my mentor, and its fruit manifested. Once again, I must admit I was somewhat afraid to talk to my manager about another new opportunity. This time, I was not leaving the office for a week; this opportunity would leave her without a secretary. Nervously I knocked on her door and breached the conversation. She paused and looked at me but not out of hatred: it was more like saying goodbye to a daughter going off to college. Perhaps they may come back home, and maybe they will not; either way, the nest was empty, and things were about to change.

Despite how she may have felt about me leaving, though I saw no indication of negativity associated with her feelings, she gave me her blessing once again. This time I had mixed emotions. I was taking a position at a different location, about thirty miles from our office. I did not have the luxury of her comfort. It was time for me to shine on my own, and doubt began to surface. At this new job, I only had the luxury of training with the person leaving the job for just one day. I found it most challenging to keep up with someone who had done the job for seventeen years. There was just no way possible for me to understand, but I sat there determined not to allow this chance to pass me by without at least trying.

In this role, I worked as an acting budget analyst. I had learned a little about budgeting in my previous job when the staff member responsible for it left for a long detail out of our department, and my manager asked me if I would be willing to handle our budget. That was in addition to my already-heavy workload without extra pay. Not knowing how to say no, I told her, "Sure," knowing it was a job out of my element.

I did everything I could to avoid math in college, a subject I had stopped loving in ninth grade. I found the job tedious and unfulfilling, yet I recalled a story of Oprah Winfrey signing all her paychecks. I learned as much as I could about it, and one of my beautiful coworkers told me the story of how she was stressed at work because she had tight writing deadlines. She did not like it and was tempted to see the negative side of the workload, but she would say to herself, "God is teaching me how to write quicker." Little did she know she would one day be the communications specialist, working directly with senior officers. Her words gave me the courage and necessary mental adjustment to do the job.

As I began to do the job, my peers commented that they would never do a job they did not get paid to do. I disagreed with the concept; I felt it would one day pay off for me if I would only be patient. I was sowing seed into my future, and I remembered the seeds you sow are the ones that grow. The scripture tells us in Galatians 6:9 (NLT), "So let's not get tired of doing what is good. At just the right time we will reap a harvest of blessing if we don't give up." I trusted that Word to manifest in my life, and finally, it did.

I had a budgeting and event management background, which made me a perfect fit for the detail. I came to work eager to make the most out of this situation. I loved most parts of the job, except for the budget. I met with industry leaders, saw a conference center renovated, engaged with internal and external clients, and even learned about the program sponsored by our team to train our next leaders. That was a slice of heaven on earth for me.

In this job, I even had a chance to step out of my personal comfort zones. My new manager and I had received an invitation to visit a hotel in New York, and I was ashamed to tell her I had never flown on an airplane. It was two years after 9/11, so I was not super enthusiastic about getting on a plane, but I did it anyway. It was a beautiful experience, and I thought I could do it again with no problems. She knew nothing about my past trouble with heights. That subject was counterproductive to my ambition, so I buried it deep inside. Thankful that I got off the plane safely, it wasn't long before I had to fly again, but this time not without event.

We had a business meeting in the midwest, which I was happy to attend. That was my second business trip. I was moving on up the ladder. As we began, we had a layover in Chicago. I had an eerie feeling all day about the flight but was afraid to tell my manager because of what she may think of me. We boarded the plane headed to Oklahoma, and my mind could not help but think I was going to die that day. I stepped onto the plane, sick to my stomach, praying the whole way, "Lord, if this plane is going to crash, please do not let it take off." We entered the runway to take off, and I prayed again, "Lord, in the name of Jesus, please, if this plane is going to crash, please don't let it take off." We sat there for a longer time than usual, and I was practically in tears.

"Ladies and Gentlemen," I heard over the speakers, "there seems to be a mechanical issue with this plane, so we are going to have to deplane you until we can get another plane."

I took a sigh of relief and praised God for answering my prayer. My manager knew I was a Christian, but she did not know I was that type of Christian. I did not want her to think I was foolish, so I did not tell her my premonitions. We got off the plane, and about an hour later, we boarded a new one. As I took my seat, the feeling came back to me again. *Are these just my nerves, or is this it for me,* I thought to myself. "Lord, I can't shake this feeling. Please, if this plane is going to crash, please, please, don't let it take off," I prayed once more. Then I heard:

"Ladies and gentlemen, we are sorry for the inconvenience, but we are having issues with the door on this plane. At this time, we are giving you vouchers to stay at a hotel near the airport, and we will book you for a flight first thing in the morning."

I went to the hotel room and fell on my knees. I praised God for sparing my life. I was too shaken to enjoy the hotel. I turned the TV to Christian Television and fell asleep. I woke up and heard a preacher talking about being obedient to the leading of the Holy Spirit and how something like that could keep you out of a plane crash. I could not believe my ears. That was no coincidence. The prompting of the Holy Spirit had spared my life that day.

In the Bible, a young boy named Samuel would one day grow to be a mighty prophet of Israel. His mother, Hannah, was one of the wives of a great man. Though she had everything she could ask for, considering she had to share her husband with another wife (indicative of the marital practices of those times), she could not have a baby. The barrenness of her womb took her joy from her. And though I am sure she was grateful for the favor she had with her husband, the other wife never let her forget her plight. It was her badge of honor and Hannah's greatest shame; barrenness of any kind brings about sadness.

Like many of us today, Hannah was grieved in her spirit at waiting for something to happen for so long and coming up empty every time. What made matters worse were she had a rival flaunting her blessings, which became a painful reminder each time she tried to no avail. She complained to her husband, and secretly she most likely felt anger toward God. Broken to her core, Hannah was one prayer away from experiencing a breakthrough that would change the course of her life and her nation, Israel. First Samuel 1:10–11 tells us, "Hannah was greatly distressed, and she prayed to the Lord and wept in anguish. She made a vow, saying, "O Lord of hosts, if You will indeed look on the affliction (suffering) of Your maidservant and remember, and not forget Your maidservant, but will give Your maidservant a son, then I will give him to the Lord all the days of his life; a razor shall never touch his head." (AMP)

Hannah dedicated this young baby to the Lord and kept her word. As soon as he came of age, she took him to the temple to honor her vows. By the time this young prophet was thirteen, he had learned to recognize, listen to, and obey the voice of God under the guidance of his teacher, Eli, the priest. The Lord honored His relationship with Samuel as he grew, and as a result, not one of the words he ever spoke in the name of the Lord failed to come to pass. In biblical days, only a few people were chosen to hear the voice of the Lord. Once Jesus came, He made that possible for all who will believe.

Though initially struggling with deciphering whether the voice is our own thought or a spiritual prompting from the Holy One, we can always be sure that He will never go against His written Word. There was no written Word for me to verify my thoughts about the airplane crashing, but like Samuel, I had spent enough time with Him to recognize that what I was feeling was not coming from my imagination. Though I honestly did not know how to handle the situation at work, I did know God knew, so I went to Him to ask Him to intervene. Thankfully, He quickly answered my prayer.

The next day we finally boarded the plane to go to our destination. We experienced turbulence at a level that scared me to the point of screaming, and I did not care that my manager was on the plane with me. She helped me calm down. If only she knew about the spiritual struggle I had about getting a glimpse of what could have been tragic for both of us. When we finally got back from that trip, I wanted to kiss the ground. I realized we should watch what we ask for because we might just get it. I wanted glory, but I did not know everything I would have to do to get there.

That year of working as a budget analyst stretched me, and sometimes I began to miss my small beginnings. There I had an opportunity to grow without the demands and pressures of unreasonable deadlines on an untrained person. It never dawned on me to ask God for help. I asked Him to protect me on the plane but not to give me the wisdom to do my job. As a result of this struggle, when the position was permanently filled, I had made too many mistakes to be considered. It was a temporary-to-permanent detail, which I was not quite ready to do full-time. I was unripe fruit. I overheard my manager say, "She has some things, but something is not quite there."

I was not mature enough to handle the job, but I was willing to learn. When I was told I would not be hired, my first instinct was to get mad, not praise God, or handle it in a positive manner. I handled it like a human who did not appreciate *not* getting the job she had worked very hard to do. I felt overlooked, and those old insecurities began to creep back up. On the one hand, I was this spiritual person many looked up to; on the other hand, I struggled with my humanity and had no proper understanding of how to reconcile the two—at least not in a way that brought honor to God. I could not get past the emotions of feeling rejected once again or the humiliation of having to go back to my secretary's desk. The hiring manager was compassionate and not a hard person to work for; she just had high expectations. After all, it was a job, not a charity event. She was not handing out jobs just because it was a nice thing to do; you had to earn it.

Not tone-deaf to the need for good mentors in our organization, she kept me on for another year to support her executive development team. That is where I began to shine the brightest. My work there got me recognized and helped to rebuild my confidence. I built more relationships and learned how to navigate the administrative side of onsite training. This newfound skillset was necessary for where I was about to go in my career. At times, I found myself grumbling about my job title, once again struggling with the pride of life. Ultimately, I learned the Lord indeed orders our steps. When we lean to our own understanding of things, we tend to come to the wrong conclusion about a matter. In an instant, we can make decisions that are not supported by a clear view of the process or the desired outcome.

When I became an event coordinator, one of the strategies I used to plan my events was to understand what the customer wanted to achieve. My role was to figure out how to get there. Once I understood the ultimate vision, I started from the end to the beginning and established a timeline and roadmap to light the way. If I knew a customer wanted to set up a function during a specific time of the month, I could not even get a venue without first researching what would be happening during that time. There are always moving parts to any project. One small thing could cause a ripple effect that might push a deadline and budget far beyond the projected cost and completion date; I learned this the hard way.

When working as a temporary employee, I was once responsible for completing some correspondence, which required a time-sensitive notification to the unions before sending information out. This notification had contractual obligations in which the specialist worked diligently to get all the proper signatures to meet the deadline established by the senior officers. My small role was formatting and mailing the signed document via registered mail. Sixty days after the letter was to be sent, we noticed a big uproar with the unions. Everyone was frantic about this correspondence. I had a filed copy of it, so I was confident it was not my fault.

While I was preparing similar notifications, I pulled out my stack of envelopes to prepare them for mailing. To my utter shock, I found the infamous letter I had so confidently guaranteed them I had sent out. My heart sank. That was truly one of the biggest tests I had ever encountered in my young Christian walk. Should I keep it to myself and let the specialist, the mailroom, or postal workers take the blame, or confess it and let the consequences associated with it fall on me was my temptation. I lost my appetite and stayed up all night worrying about it. I knew I could not afford to lose my job. I was barely making any money with my little salary, and honestly, I just could not take another loss at that time. I prayed about it and was really hoping I could just repent and be done. It would just be between God and me, but the conviction I had in the matter would not let me do it. I desired more than anything to please God, so I confessed.

"This is the hardest thing I have ever had to do in my career, but I must do it anyway. While preparing my envelopes to mail my other correspondences, I realized I must have inadvertently packed your envelopes with the unused ones when I cleaned up my desk. Please forgive me; I am so sorry," I said with tears in my eyes. The man took a lot of heat for my mistake, but he offered me mercy, which is the very thing I asked of God. He used my mistake as a teachable moment and helped me understand we all mess up, but he was very proud that I had told him the truth. Though still embarrassed about my shortcoming, I became respected in the eyes of those who knew of my story, even though that one little mistake created confusion and caused the program to be delayed another sixty days.

That lesson helped me appreciate the importance of the moving parts in a job, but I could not connect those dots in my private life. I did not totally comprehend what it meant for God to be the Potter in our lives. Perhaps I could not grasp this concept because I am a visual learner. I needed to realize the clay does not tell a potter how to create it, but the potter has an idea and shapes and models the vessel until it's complete. The whole pottery process is intriguing. It goes through a physical and chemical transformation. It begins wet and then is polished and ultimately put into the fire to finish. When preached, it sounds like an inspirational message but is oh so painful when taken from theory to practicum.

My thought process about how long it was taking me to achieve my dreams was in line with the Lord's rebuke in Jeremiah 18:1–6 (KJV):

> "The word which came to Jeremiah from the Lord, saying, Arise, and go down to the potter's house, and there I will cause thee to hear my words. Then I went down to the potter's house, and behold, he wrought a work on the wheels. And the vessel that he made of clay was marred in the hand of the potter: so he made it again another vessel, as seemed good to the potter to make it. Then the word of the Lord came to me, saying, O house of Israel, cannot I do with you as this potter? saith the Lord. Behold, as the clay is in the potter's hand, so are ye in mine hand, O house of Israel."

The Potter was undoubtedly at work in me, and I was about to realize just how great His plan was for my life. About a year into my work as a training specialist, it was time to return to my original job as a secretary. I had been away from that job for two years and did not want to go back. Feeling depressed about the end of what I thought was a position with promise, I struggled to keep my countenance together. Once again, my beautiful mentor helped me see the blessing behind what I had just experienced, and though I was still sad, it was good to be back in the comfort of her leadership.

Our department was assigned a massive project, one of which would change the innovation of our Human Resources (HR) processes. We were creating a center that would be a centralized place to process all our HR transactions for the entire organization. The mission was accomplished by recruiting the subject matter experts in their field to provide feedback, testing, and structure for this monumental task. We had a project team meeting to kick off this project at the center where I had just served for the past two years, and as a secretary, I was tasked to take notes and provide administrative support to the team.

While at the meeting, we had trouble with our meeting room and needed to get it fixed quickly. The conference center was full of other customers, so we had to wait until someone could get in touch with the support team. I saw an opportunity to fix this problem, and I jumped in with enthusiasm. Since I knew the team, their direct numbers, and where they were at any given time, I was able to get them to help me. I ran to my old office, called the IT people on the walkie-talkie, and had them prioritize my request.

When they found out it was me, they were up there within minutes, and quickly our project went off without any further issues. I felt useful, needed, and appreciated. My former teammates greeted me with smiles and hugged me when they saw me, and the staff attending the meeting saw a person who knew how to get results quickly. The smile on my manager's face made me feel as if she was proud of me. When we got back to the office the next day, we did our usual meeting debriefs, but this time it came with an opportunity I did not see coming.

"Angela, the team lead, has requested you to work on the team in Minnesota. You will be needed for two days out there." *Wow!* Smiling from ear to ear, I could hardly wait to tell my mother. "Of course, I would love to do something like that," I told her. In August, I flew out to Minnesota for two days and did such a good job that I received permission to be a permanent team member. Six months later, I had earned so many frequent flyer miles that the airlines automatically upgraded me to first class on most of my flights. I became genuinely good friends with the hotel staff and was a part of the highest-performing team I had seen in my career. From day one, we all got along. We ate together, toured the city together, and created a system that would one day be the benchmark for other companies to follow.

This outcome became a center of excellence, and I was a part of it. I won awards, received public recognition, and gained experience that only one other secretary in our organization was getting at that time. As the project was ending, I was ready to go home. Catching the red-eye to Minnesota first thing Monday mornings and flying out late Friday evenings to return home for six months straight ultimately took its toll on my body. I was tired and simply happy to be getting back to my family.

Before completing the detail in Minnesota, I was never home during the week. Still, they allowed me to briefly return home to go on a job interview and honor our retiring inspirational leader and vice president. Under his leadership, I developed my wings to fly; I could not allow him to leave without saying goodbye. Before he left, he hugged me and told me he expected to hear great things from me. He was the type of leader you were willing to go the extra mile for because he believed in you, and you believed in him.

After the retirement party, I had a job interview for a higher-level entry staff position. The questions asked at this interview were easy to answer because my unique collective experience aligned perfectly with the duties of the job and the department's strategic goals. I left that interview feeling confident in my answers yet excited to get back to Minnesota and finish my assignment so I could finally permanently return home. I said my goodbyes to the team and reflected on the good times I had in the city with 10,000 lakes. Though the external weather was freezing cold and constantly below zero, my team made the experience warm and cozy with their professionalism and kindness.

As the youngest member of the team, I learned to appreciate the veterans in an organization. If you respected them and honored the years of their experience without coming to them, thinking you knew it all, they would reward you with enough nuggets to ensure you knew more than the person not invited to sit at their table. A seasoned employee once told me, "I'll teach you everything you know, but I will not teach you everything I know."

Their lessons proved to be quite useful in my career progression, and it was about to pay off generously. As I arrived back at Reagan National Airport, I checked my voicemail messages in the car as I was leaving out the parking garage and heard, "Angela, congratulations, I would like to offer you the job." I sat in the car overjoyed by that voicemail to the point I heard someone blowing their horn behind me as it was my turn to pay the attendant. "I'm sorry," I told the attendant. "I just got some great news. I got a promotion, and I am so happy about it!"

It was nice to see a stranger share that joy with me. Too bad I did not receive the same jubilation from my peers. When people started noticing my star shining, I began to lose some of those I held near and dear to my heart. Sadly enough, I did not understand what I was seeing. It bothered me deeply when I realized I had the respect of the leaders but not the people who were once my peers. I was thought of like a brown noser because I wanted to get to know the managers. I had a decision to make: I could either allow their opinions of me to derail my future or to move on without their support, and that's what I did exactly.

People I had once prayed for and with began to turn their backs on me. It was a hard lesson to learn about power and its provocation of jealousy in the hearts of those who craved it. As a young Christian, I could not fathom that people you care about could turn on you if you dared to be more than what they thought you should be. Ambitious people seem to intimidate those who have settled in the bosom of comfortability. To reach higher heights, one must stretch themselves beyond the status quo. Any place a person can be in that becomes stagnant is a representation of the Dead Sea: full of good things. Still, the stagnation of the water causes an accumulation of minerals too toxic for the survival of any life form.

Once I recognized the hostility I was beginning to experience because of my newfound success, I focused on learning my job and providing excellent customer service, and I made some new friends along the way. Life was good for me; I had a great team and a job I began to love. This job exposed me to industry CEOs, leaders, and employees around the country and even more opportunities to travel to different places. I was living my dream, but life is full of peaks and valleys, and I was about to experience both simultaneously.

My mother had experienced some issues with her stomach and decided to go to the doctor for some diagnostic tests. When I took her to this appointment, I was not aware of what they were testing her for or why she had to be put to sleep to do it. I looked around in the waiting room and saw the word *oncology*. I knew that word from the days of working at the hospital. Once she came out, I asked why we were in there? "They just wanted to take a look at my stomach," she said quietly.

When the word came back that my mother had stage two stomach cancer, I could not grasp that concept. My heart could not have been more broken. On the one hand, I was a rising star at work, and on the other, I was facing my mother's mortality. I prayed with everything in me, crying out to the Lord to heal my mother.

My mother, BJ, as people affectionately knew her, was a prayer warrior with a tremendous love of life. Her sense of humor and storytelling gained her friends from every walk of life. A self-proclaimed cowgirl, this lady's sense of adventure often got her into trouble with her parents, growing up. We would be around the dinner table, listening to her siblings talk about her antics, and marveled at the fact that they all lived to tell the story. From making homemade kayaks to riding my grandfather's pigs, to having the strength to chop wood with the same vigor or better than the boys in the family, this woman was a pillar of strength.

Mom often took offense to people calling her John Henry, the strongest steel driver for the railroad. This time, no matter how strong she was, physically and spiritually, cancer was a formidable opponent in her fight for life. The doctors told her she had to undergo aggressive chemotherapy, surgery, and chemotherapy again. I never saw a moment in my mother's life where fear began to grip her, but courageously she set out to take on a battle that had defeated many people worldwide. She knew one thing for sure; this emergency did not spark her prayer life. She had a solid relationship with God, and she felt peace in knowing the situation was just a continuation of daily conversations she had with the Lord.

Together, along with the love and support of her children and siblings, we came up with a plan to help her through her challenge. Since I was living near her and my siblings were out of state, I would be the one to take Family Medical Leave to care for her during her healing. I did not know what to expect, but I saw God move in her life most miraculously. I initially tried to convince my mom to pray about it and just believe God for a miracle, and she told me, "Sometimes God gives you a miracle, and that miracle can come from the wisdom He has given doctors." She acknowledged she had cancer, but she also determined she would do whatever the doctors advised her to do for it to go into remission. My thought process was not remission but total healing, but I understood how forcing my thoughts on someone facing their mortality was not helpful but condescending. It came across as "That's the wrong approach; believe this way. Perhaps you should strengthen your faith."

The last thing a caregiver should want to do is make a patient feel condemned for their response to illness. I apologized for my pushy ways, acquiesced to her approach, and provided care for her from that vantage point. Being on the same page as my mother was instrumental in her recovery. Taking her cues on what she needed me to do and learning to support her in a manner that made her feel safe is an approach I would recommend to any caregiver.

At times caregiving was overwhelming, but my heart was to show her that she was not a burden to me. Often people who feel like burdens to their caregivers have little incentive for fighting for their lives. It creates an environment ripe for giving up. There were long nights and emotional trauma in watching my mother suffer, but I was determined not to allow the stress from my job and the tiredness of my body to show on my face when serving her.

My vice president at the time was a cool and very well-put-together leader. He gave me the freedom to take care of my mother, using an alternative work schedule, which included me sometimes working into the night. The flexibility I experienced allowed me to run my nationwide program from my mother's hospital bed without missing a beat. The type of treatment my mother had to go through to fight this rare cancer required her to receive twenty-four hours of chemotherapy and major flushing of stronger chemo every twenty-one days. The pain from that alone was tough on my mother, but having to have 60 percent of her stomach and a portion of her esophagus removed and then return to the same grueling chemo treatment took its toll on her emotionally.

> "Mom, the doctor said you have to eat in order not to die from malnutrition," I explained to her with much concern in my heart.
>
> "I just can't eat, Baby," she told me as I looked at her plate and saw a small bite from a cracker and another from the cheese.

I knew she could not survive long on that caloric intake. At her next follow-up appointment, the doctor asked her about her eating. Anxious to get a tube removed from her stomach, she told him it was okay. I knew my mother would not like me interjecting my voice in this scenario, but I had to tell him how she was not eating enough to survive. The look on her face told me I was going to get it when we left that office, but I did not care. I wanted results. The doctor left the feeding tube in her for the remaining of her chemo treatments, and as she would rest, I would fill her IV with a prescribed food supplement to give her the strength to recover. Initially, she was angry with my decision to speak about her health but began to see the wisdom in it.

Mom opted to return to work with a twenty-four-hour chemo bag on her chest to create some normalcy in her life. The combination of the first round of chemo, the surgery, and the last round caused side effects, including foot and mouth ulcers. I watched my mother commute to her job twenty-five miles away to do a job she had always dreamed of doing. As an account manager, she was responsible for attending to the needs of small business clients. Despite her challenges, she visited embassies, organizations, churches, and small businesses throughout three states and the District of Columbia. She held open enrollment fairs and interfaced with customers as frequently as physically possible. She attended those events driving her car while often unable to eat because of sores inside her mouth and could hardly stand on the hard organizational floor because of the sores on her feet. Still, she never let her customer see her pain.

Perhaps she did encompass the spirit of John Henry, but I know her strength came from the Lord. As the chemo days accumulated and the stress of her deadlines began to contribute to chronic fatigue, I noticed a sadness in my mother. She was never a person to complain about how she felt, so to see her get strangely quiet was troubling. Was she giving up? Was she hiding news about her condition? Whatever the case, I started talking to her about prayer.

> "Mom, let's pray."
>
> "Not right now," she told me. After several offers of prayer, met with the same response, I knew something was amiss.
>
> "What's wrong, Mom?"
>
> "I don't know; I just can't pray."

I thank God that He gave me the wisdom to respond to her with love instead of condemnation. "Mom, they tell you about the physical aspect that comes with this diagnosis, but they did not adequately prepare us for the spiritual or emotional toll this would have on you. I'll pray for you instead," I offered.

At that point, I understood that we could all go through moments where we felt weak. Without wanting to verbalize it, Mom felt disappointed in the trial she was experiencing. Her inability to pray for herself during that time inspired me to pray for her even harder. I did this in addition to working a demanding job and still trying to keep a level of ambition within my heart. Her sickness often left me contemplating our spiritual journey.

When we learn to pray, speak the Word of God, fast, and live a "Spirit-filled" Christian life, we realize another layer of pride is waiting there for us—the pride of being invincible, as if nothing could ever make us struggle with unbelief or the frustration of being in situations we did not see coming. We develop a false sense of security when we rely on the concept that our works and obedience will somehow make us exempt from ever seeing tribulation. Jesus tells us in 1 Peter 4:12–13 (KJV), "Beloved, think it not strange concerning the fiery trial which is to try you, as though some strange thing happened unto you: but rejoice, inasmuch as ye are partakers of Christ's sufferings; that, when his glory shall be revealed, ye may be glad also with exceeding joy."

My mother's condition taught me the importance of having a circle of believers who would pray for you when you needed it most. In the Gospels, there is a story about a paralyzed man whose friends had faith for him when he could not move. Mark 2:1–12 (NKJV) teaches:

"And again He entered Capernaum after *some* days, and it was heard that He was in the house. Immediately many gathered together so that there was no longer room to receive *them,* not even near the door. And He preached the word to them. Then they came to Him, bringing a paralytic who was carried by four *men*. And when they could not come near Him because of the crowd, they uncovered the roof where He was. So when they had broken through, they let down the bed on which the paralytic was lying. When Jesus saw their faith, He said to the paralytic, "Son, your sins are forgiven you. And some of the scribes were sitting there and reasoning in their hearts, "Why does this *Man* speak blasphemies like this? Who can forgive sins but God alone?" But immediately, when Jesus perceived in His spirit that they reasoned thus within themselves, He said to them, "Why do you reason about these things in your hearts? Which is easier, to say to the paralytic, '*Your* sins are forgiven you,' or to say, 'Arise, take up your bed and walk?' But that you may know that the Son of Man has [b]power on earth to forgive sins." He said to the paralytic, "I say to you, arise, take up your bed, and go to your house." Immediately he arose, took up the bed, and went out in the presence of them all, so that all were amazed and glorified God, saying, "We never saw *anything* like this!"

It did not matter to me that my mother could not pray for herself; my only concern was that Jesus would hear my prayers and heal her. The Lord honored my heartfelt request to heal my mother, and I grew immensely because of it. Personally, I began to see that I was way too judgmental and, at times, obnoxious about my faith. Professionally, I learned how the strength and support of a team could help its team members go and grow through the most trying seasons of their personal life. My work performance reflected my growth during this time. Using my mother's dedication as a roadmap to my work ethic got me promoted to a higher grade in my office. Soon after that, I was recruited for another promotion in a different department. My star continued rising, but a star shines brightest in dark places.

Dark Night of the Soul

"When it rains, it pours." —Morton Salt Company

Anyone who has ever served as a caregiver can relate to what it does to your soul. Watching your loved ones suffer slowly breaks you down. Unfortunately, you often don't realize how wounded you are because you have programmed yourself to operate in automatic mode, also known as the schedule. Once the person you have cared for is no longer in need of your services, you notice all the things you neglected along the way; at least, that's how it was for me.

Once my mother received a cancer-free report, I should have taken that time to dissect my feelings, but the cares of this world did not allow me to do so. I didn't take the time to adjust my schedule to add self-care because the carrot of success was dangling in front of me, and I had to obtain it. My mother told me I would always be blessed because of how well I took care of her, and I was beginning to see signs of significant positive changes manifest in my life.

I loved the professional doors God was opening for me. I thought I was aligned with His will because I went to church and praised Him. On May 28, 2004, I learned that God had a different plan for my life. I attended a worship service where a pastor known for great prophetic insight preached. Not long into the service, he called me up to the front and told me the Lord had a book for me to write, and I was taking my time doing it. Of course, I was excited about the message confirming one of my dreams, but I was embarrassed because I knew I was taking my time. When you are young, there is a tendency to think you have all the time in the world to do things. You will do it someday, one day, later.

The scriptures tell us in Ephesians 5:11–16 (MSG):

Don't waste your time on useless work, mere busywork, the barren pursuits of darkness. Expose these things for the sham they are. It's a scandal when people waste their lives on things they must do in the darkness where no one will see. Rip the cover off those frauds and see how attractive they look in the light of Christ. Wake up from your sleep. Climb out of your coffins; Christ will show you the light! So watch your step. Use your head. Make the most of every chance you get. These are desperate times!"

I was about to learn the folly of living in the hopes of tomorrow. As a reminder, I purchased the CD of that night's message. I walked around like a spiritual peacock because I had a word from the Lord. He publicly told everyone about my book, and of course, it left me beaming. However, life is full of distractions, and mine was pursuing success. Whenever things got bad for me, I would think about the night the Lord deposited a prophetic word in my heart. Since I had a Plan B, I felt unfazed about the struggles of work. I had the attitude that I would one day do what the Lord asked me to do, so I did not care that I didn't like everything about my job. The money was good, and I had another plan, but there is no Plan B whenever God gives us a directive.

About two years after receiving the instructions to write, I still made no progress. I attended a church service in Minnesota, and the preacher spoke about understanding the Holy Spirit. In his message, he inadvertently said, "I bet if things got rough for you at work, you would write that book." I could run, but I could not hide from the instruction of God. It was not enough for me to hear the Word, but I had to do it to see it manifest in my life. Isaiah 1:19 (NKJV) says, "If you are willing and obedient, you will eat the good of the land." Hearing the preacher that cold night in Minnesota caused me to tremble at the thought of entering any kind of hard times at work. Then I got busy climbing the ladder with my eyes set on having a brick with my name on it at our leadership center. I was deceiving myself, just like the scriptures said in the book of James.

James 1:22–24 (MSG) teaches, "Don't fool yourself into thinking that you are a listener when you are anything but, letting the Word go in one ear and out the other. *Act* on what you hear! Those who hear and don't act are like those who glance in the mirror, walk away, and two minutes later have no idea who they are, what they look like."

My focus was not on fulfilling God's purpose but achieving my dreams. Soon, I advanced in a new position that gave me greater leverage to the path of the highest office, chief executive officer. I did not care what people thought of me; I had plans to be the first African American to hold that office. The thing about pride and the believer is it's never God's desire for us to seek after prestige, but rather to seek Him and His ways, and He will give us what we need. Matthew 6:33 (AMP), "But first *and* most importantly seek (aim at, strive after) His kingdom and His righteousness [His way of doing and being right—the attitude and character of God], and all these things will be given to you also."

Since I was a volunteer spiritual director for a prison, an intercessor prayer warrior, a caregiver, and a Sunday school teacher, I honestly did not see the wrong in my pursuits, but delayed obedience is disobedience. Even the busiest and most pious child of God will have to answer to the spots on their robe, no matter how big or how small.

I had become quite busy trying to balance my career with my spiritual compass. I met a physical trainer at my previous job, and we became good friends. He invited me to his congregation. I went there, and I can honestly say those believers supported me tremendously when my mother was sick. Their pastor was a wonderful man of God for whom I will always have tremendous love, along with his wife. I was given many opportunities to serve the Lord at this church. For the first time in my life, everything was falling into place, but I still did not attempt to obey the instruction to write.

I belonged to a Toastmasters club at work, and I started speaking and winning competitions around the city. A speaker's bureau recruited me at one event, and I began getting paid to do motivational speaking. Still, I did not do what the Lord told me to do. Even more, I had a new love interest, a boutique apartment in the city on the eleventh floor, my car was paid off, my credit was good, my ministry was also growing, and I had just gotten accepted into an Advanced Leadership Program (reserved for only the top performers slated for entering the executive ranks). Life was good, and there was no sense of urgency to do what the Lord said—no disrespect to Him, just taking my time.

As the financial crisis hit many organizations in our country, we also had our economic hardships—our solution was a reduction in force. It wasn't only the ark that saved Noah from the flood; it was his timely obedience to building it. Though he had never seen rainfall, he prepared for the rainy day at the guidance of God. I was completely unprepared for a monsoon of trouble that was about to come crashing down on my life. In any big organization, you will have great leaders and mediocre managers. Leadership is more than casting a vision and steering a ship. It's about selling your company's vision at such a level that everyone falls into place to play their role. To be more than a presentation of glossy words requires thought and intention. If the leader is not whole, the organization will reflect their weakness. It's not only the mirrors of a car that a driver must consider, but also their blind spots. The corporate employee survey is always there to tell you how the employees are doing and if they need some tender love and care (TLC).

Often tenderness, love, and caring are not synonymous with work. Unfortunately, we live in a society where people think you should just be happy to have a job. Once my manager delivered me a survey and told me to be careful what I wrote because my vice president knew I gave the feedback. I understood that as they did not want my genuine opinion but a high positive score. In that case, there was no possible way the organization wanted to improve its treatment of its employees; they were in survival mode and just trying to stay afloat.

I decided to make it my life's work to create a culture that embraced and encouraged everyone to do their best. If I could operate an employee program from my mother's ICU bed, I could inspire my department in the area of employee engagement and thus began my downfall. My lofty thoughts about getting along and creating camaraderie became my passion, although my life was falling apart personally.

Prior to meeting the man I thought I was going to marry, I met a gentleman I considered my soulmate. He was not a man of Christian faith, but his integrity,intelligence, and self-discipline stirred my heart. Though he did not agree with my convictions, he maintained a sense of decency with me whenever we conversed. He was honest about his life and treated me with great respect. Though I was disappointed at not being able to get to know this man on a romantic level, I had met a real gentleman and was happy to do so. Not long after, I wondered if I would ever find love. If I could meet a man with whom I had so much in common that did not amount to anything, where else could my life partner be? Everyone knew I was single and wanted to see me with a husband. I had a great career, was buying a house, growing in ministry, and doing better than most financially, but I had no children or husband, so my life was not complete in the eyes of some.

A friend at church told me about a man interested in me and we started dating. Right when I was closing on my house, we began to experience trouble from which we never recovered. His friends taunted him for dating someone outside of his race, and his daughter moved out of the country. Together, those things became too much for him to bear. What I thought was a beautiful love story turned into a nightmare. I was in a Dr. Jekyll and Mr. Hyde relationship. There were red flags everywhere to get out; one such flag included having several tormenting dreams of us together.

I was happy to see my finances flourish enough to buy a house in the city. God blessed me to pay no money down and no closing costs for my new home, customized to my liking. It was supposed to be a time of celebration. The man of my dreams had proposed to me, and I said yes, but after his daughter left, he was in deep pain, and I was the recipient of that trauma. We spent the next three years breaking up and getting back together with no apparent resolution in sight. Our arguments were so volatile that the relationship began to affect my health. For the first time in my life, I dealt with blood pressure issues. There is a saying that there is a thin line between love and hate. We are taught not to hate in the Christian world, but I can tell you I honestly started to feel that emotion. I could not understand how something so beautiful could turn so ugly, but then I realized obedience is better than sacrifice.

When we begin to cross those lines, we see the consequences of our decisions. Everything is about choices in life. What I learned from that relationship is that it is better to be with someone who tells you the truth than to be with someone who lies. When they lie to you about their intention, feelings, and love for you, it is far more damaging than accepting the truth from a person telling you they are not ready or interested in pursuing any meaningful relationship.

The person who told me the truth about his intentions was not a Christian, however, he still had respect for the God in me. The person I chose at church had me thinking that just because he raised his hands to praise God and sang songs so beautifully and had a working knowledge of the Bible, he was a man of great honor. The dishonorable way he treated me began to put significant breaks in my heart. Sadly enough, instead of walking away from him, I began to see a pattern of abuse when I allowed him to continue his behavior.

Still hurting from my mother's battle with cancer and now dealing with an unhealthy relationship, I turned to work to try to find some peace but to no avail. My vice president asked me to join her staff as a direct report. She told me she would not give me a staff, but my job depended on my ability to influence the people who worked indirectly for me.

No one wants to have multiple people telling them what to do in any organization. I knew I had no real power to make the employees do the work I had assigned them, but I had to find a way to do it with pizzazz. I used my method of building relationships with people to get the job done. Whenever I would receive an award, I made it a point to share it with my team. After a successful event, I would bake them cakes or buy them lunch. I even invited them over to my house for dinner. Not wanting to sound the alarm about my leadership approach, I did not inform my vice president about my strategy. I just got the job done.

Inspirational leadership will most likely earn you the respect of those who support you. My team would often come in early, stay late, and spend their money working on my creative vision for our major town hall events. My goal was to produce town hall events to improve the organizational culture. Due to our budget restraints and several reductions in force, we saw employees do more with less. This workload did nothing to enhance corporate morale.

I knew how employees felt about their company, boss, or work could significantly impact how they interfaced with customers, ultimately affecting the bottom line. I took the data on our dignity and respect question from our survey and set out to improve those scores. We had two significant gatherings twice a year, and I knew this was my time to seize the moment. The reduction in force had left a coldness in the office. I proposed a winter wonderland–themed event to warm the place up.

When I was justifying my reasons for that theme, I watched as my coworkers laughed and mocked me because I wanted to make things better. I was very offended by this but knew I had to keep my composure to fulfill my vision. We transformed a room with white decorations, played good music, and ate good food, all with zero budget. We had a person on my staff with a catering company, and he provided the silverware and catered food containers and burners. I borrowed tablecloths from the events department, and my creative coworkers made snowflakes out of paper and filled the room with them. The centerpieces for the table were snowmen and snow villages from our own homes, and a teammate who moonlighted as a DJ provided music. My staff agreed to wear all winter white, which was the beginning of what I called "The Funky Town Halls." The creative, cost-effective potluck business meetings became the talk of the building. We did them so professionally that people started asking to see our budget report to ensure we were not spending during the budget freeze.

When I was asked to be a cross-functional manager with no staff, I took that job seriously. Developing my ability to influence was why I received the job, so things going sour for me was very confusing. I became very beloved in the building by those in grade levels below me. My office was a revolving door of people coming to talk to me about the different challenges they had with their bosses. I used this information to build a better culture, but some above me did not agree with my popularity. My boss called me into the office one day, seemingly annoyed by my existence.

She pointed her finger at me and said, "My problem with you is that you are not the b-word."

"Everyone has different leadership styles," I told her.

She looked me in the eye and said, "If I'm calling you in the office, I don't see any."

Stunned, I did not know what was happening. I improved scores, got results, met deadlines, and was the least respected person on our team. I noticed I was not given new work. Frequently, I sat in my office, trying to find something to do. A loyal coworker came and told me "rumor had it" that I was going to rot in that office. I was beyond disturbed at this notation but started to see the truth in it. I wish I could say I was okay, but I was not. I instantly became very delusional at the job and the company I had served for nearly twenty years. Having people walk by my office looking in there, knowing I was not being assigned work, was a hard pill to swallow. Occasionally, when there was an event or budget meeting, I was able to work then, but my brand and all the good vibes and awards I had won went up in smoke.

The words spoken to me about not having leadership skills were an attack on my character. I had been a leader since elementary school, serving as captain of the school guard traffic safety patrols. I was also captain of my band section in high school, in the pep club, and executive officer of my JROTC Army Battalion. At Bennett, I served as the resident hall president. When I was recruited to work at that job, two weeks into my job, the team lead left during a critical time in our organization, and I volunteered to do the job in addition to mine until they could find a replacement. I arrived at work before sunrise and stayed until after sunset. Sometimes after 8:00 p.m., I was still there, praying for wisdom and learning the job. I did such an outstanding job that I was promoted within four months to the team lead position, which eventually got me appointed as a cross-functional manager. When I got that job, a man called me to warn me to be careful because if I fell out of grace with my boss, my career would be ruined. I had a tremendous amount of respect for this brilliant boss; I never thought it would happen to me.

It was time for me to leave, so I applied for a lower-level job in San Diego, CA but did not get it. I felt like David when he lost favor with King Saul. I was stuck. Everything I did from that point seemed to irritate my boss and her executives. They treated me badly, and I had no one to talk to about it. I felt my career was over, which was very traumatizing to me.

By then, I had only been in my new home for two years, and I was constantly fighting with my partner. My elders, who were my mother's siblings, began to get sick. After one of many emotional breakups with my partner, I purchased a Mercedes I couldn't afford, which was draining my finances with maintenance costs, sometimes exceeding $2,500. Our church was going through a split, and I immaturely took sides and left because I secretly resented being in the same place as the man who deeply hurt me. Suddenly, everywhere I turned was stormy, and the sun seemed so far away.

To be fair, my vice president told me I had changed, and maybe I did not see it because I was still meeting my deadlines and producing exceptional events, but there was a deep sadness in me that erased my smile. I would have loved for her to coach me like the manager who cared enough to tell me the ways she saw a difference in me, but instead, I was punished and cast away from the team, often left in the office by myself, without even a "good evening, we'll see you tomorrow."

The emotional trauma I was suffering from my relationships was ripping me apart, and not having my church as a place of refuge added fuel to that fire. I felt like a wanderer upon the earth with no place in which to rest my weary soul. I thought God was doing these things to me. He corrected me for my sins and caused me to have a hard time in life because that is what I had learned over the years about the love of God.

A leader of a prayer group, for whom I had tremendous respect, told me, "Walking with God is like walking on eggshells." His wife said that if I messed up, I would have to start all over again. I was rooted in condemnation and legalism and did not even know how deeply erroneous teaching had impacted my life. I knew I was still that girl sitting out in the rain, waiting for the doors of the church to open just to learn about God, but His people were mean, and I did not have joy in going anymore. What was once a haven had become a prison of unattainable expectations. Where the Spirit of the Lord is, there is liberty, but I was bound in the chains of the rudiments of men.

Paul admonished us in his letter to Colossians not to allow man's opinions to bind our understanding of God. Colossians 2:6–10 (NLT) tells us:

> "And now, just as you accepted Christ Jesus as your Lord, you must continue to follow Him. Let your roots grow down into Him, and let your lives be built on Him. Then your faith will grow strong in the truth you were taught, and you will overflow with thankfulness. Don't let anyone capture you with empty philosophies and high-sounding nonsense that come from human thinking and from the spiritual powers of this world, rather than from Christ. For in Christ lives all the fullness of God in a human body. So you also are complete through your union with Christ, who is the head over every ruler and authority."

Many people in this world leave the church and decide they want nothing to do with religion; I never thought I would be one of those. I eventually stopped praying like I used to and just tried my best to survive daily amid all my troubles. I remembered listening to the radio during Hurricane Katrina when I was in Minnesota. Before the storm reached landfall, citizens were told to evacuate. Many people interviewed had decided to wait it out, though warned of its destructive path. Unfortunately, it ended up being one of the most tragic hurricanes this country had ever experienced.

I became highly interested in that storm at that time because I was traveling. After the near-death experience on the airplane, I did not want to be in the air with tropical storms and tornados brewing. Everyone was talking about this pending storm. After the hurricane hit, I got into a very heated discussion with a lady. "Why didn't they just leave?" she asked smugly. "I would know what to do in that scenario." When she said that to me, I had to calm myself down because the audacity for any of us to say what we would do in any situation when we have not walked a mile in that person's shoes is beyond presumptuous. The hurricane was unpredictable, and many who were poor had nowhere to go. They were losing more than their homes; they were losing lives, family, and sadly enough, hope for a better tomorrow.

I became obsessed with learning as much as I could about that hurricane. Eventually, I dreamed about one that became a foreshadowing of the things to come for my family and me. I was at my aunt's trailer in Pantego, NC, in this dream. My family was dispersed throughout different rooms. I went to a big window and saw a storm cloud in the shape of an 18 wheeler truck rolling by our house. I knew destruction was imminent, considering the size of that storm and the instability of the trailer. Hence, I started crying, stretched my hand toward the window, and forcefully started praying.

I woke up, trembling, pondering those things in my heart. Still not completely over my relationship with the man I loved, I foolishly let him back in my life only to fall back into the pattern of breaking up to make up. The Lord sent me dreams again during these times, each one more disturbing than the next. In a different dream, I saw myself driving to my former job at our Leadership Center and was caught in a tsunami. A wave of dirty water pushed me into a house with many doors and vicious dogs outside. I tried to close them and went to one with a window. Inside the window panel was a sticker that read, "Put your hands in the hands of Jesus," and then I woke up. The night terrors I was beginning to have impacted my sleep. There was no peace at home, no peace at work, and no peace at church for me, only trouble—and it did not stop there.

My family was always remarkably close. When my mother and her siblings migrated to Washington, DC, from Washington, NC, they were given a mandate by their parents to look out for each other and to stay close, no matter what—a job they all took seriously. All eight siblings lived near each other, and the ninth one moved to Florida, but he might as well have been around the corner because he managed to keep the lines of communication open, though located so far away.

As the middle child, my mom was the youngest sibling to the four oldest children and the oldest to the four youngest children. She was either told what to do by her oldest siblings or giving orders to the youngest. Either way, she was a connector and had a special relationship with them all. Mom dedicated her entire life to her family. Her mother raised her to be strong enough to take on the world, but nothing could prepare her for the heartbreak she would face in her life.

At the turn of the twenty-first century, my mother lost two older brothers within a year. She grieved their death deeply and often thought that grief contributed to her illness. Not since losing her mother, not long after her father died, had she experienced so much pain. For thirteen years, she and her siblings dedicated their lives to building our family and making sure we could move forward in the love we had cultivated throughout the years. We faced some rocky times within those years, but we still prevailed.

As a prayer warrior, she spent countless hours praying for her family. Each time she went to the altar, she rose, thanking God for answering her prayer but still hurting over the things she had to request. Her youngest sister had been diagnosed with cancer, while her youngest brother needed a lung implant. She was still trying to recover mentally from her bout with cancer; she was grateful to be praying again, but still very fragile.

Mom got up after praying one day, knowing God answered her prayer. No less than a week later, my uncle received a call to have the lung transplant surgery, and she courageously supported him while he was recovering while also praying for her sister's terminal cancer report. We supported our mother as best we could, but I became her support system since I lived close to her. From North Carolina to Maryland, my mother would spend her weekends selflessly caring for the sick. It was heartbreaking to watch her heartbreak. Around that time, we got the call that her other sister was taking cancer tests, and her other brothers were also suffering from illnesses. It seemed like trouble was surrounding us on every end. We prayed and believed things would get better for our family, but they did not. The lungs failed in her younger brother, and we had to say goodbye. This funeral shook my family. It felt like a tremendous earthquake had ripped through our bloodline. It had been years since we said goodbye to one of our family members, which wounded us deeply.

When my uncle first started showing symptoms of his body rejecting the new lungs, my boss retired. She left the organization, but not without me putting together all the pictures I had taken of our events and honoring her before her staff. No matter what had happened between us, I learned a lot under her tutelage, and I thought she deserved a great send-off. When she saw my work, she became very emotional. I forgave her, and I can only hope she forgave me, too, because perhaps the pain I was experiencing impacted my work.

One of the things I failed to do was defend my worth and value to the team. I was just a human being behind human capital. I had problems, good days, and bad days, but I was teachable and committed. I don't blame my boss for my inability to handle everything that happened in my life with a big smile and lots of enthusiasm. To some, that's perceived as a weakness; to me, it was an opportunity to heal authentically.

I needed a space to recover from the environment, so I decided to return to the Leadership Center with hopes of a new beginning, but unfortunately, my brand had been tarnished. From day one until six months later, the manager who had lost her executive status in the reorganization was rude, condescending, mean, uncaring, and vindictive. She would make comments like "cracking the whip" to her colleagues in my presence. The people who noticed her treatment of me were afraid to speak up on my behalf. My blood pressure became so high that I was often sick. My hair started to grey, and I began to lose weight. I could not sleep, and I fell deeper and deeper into depression. She left for a few months and was replaced by a wonderful person. We got along great and did great things.

Since she removed the office away from that position and made me sit out in front of her desk like her secretary, I asked if I could decorate the place to make it more like a conference center. We had previously done a lot of renovating and painting, and I thought things were still that way. The staff brought up some paint samples, and I was set to get the space ready. After selecting the color, my uncle unexpectedly took a turn for the worse and died. They came to paint on a Friday, and I did not return to work until that Monday. When I got back in the office, the color was not as light as I thought it was, and I was not there to stop them because I was at the funeral. This woman went off on me. Though it was a soft lavender in this conference center office with brown historical pictures on the wall, they called me in the office and asked, "Have you noticed all the walls of the executive headquarters are white and none are colored?" I told them, "Actually, they are grey, and we are sitting in a yellow room now."

It was that moment when she referenced "cracking the whip" in a room full of nonblacks; I felt as if it was a racial slur because, from day one, she had been so nasty to me that I thought perhaps she was somewhat biased toward me. When I mentioned it, she said to me, "There you go pulling the race card." That was my cue to shut up about it. She wrote me up for the walls and made me pay the labor and cost of the paint. The director of facilities told me to challenge it because everyone had their office painted, but I knew I did not have a leg to stand on because it is not what you accuse people of; it's what you can prove.

After that, I left for a week and cared for my aunt dying from cancer. One month to the day after my uncle passed away, I got a call to come to the hospital because she would not make it through the night. I immediately fell apart at work. I told the manager I had to leave because of a family emergency. My aunt, who I had just returned from caring for, was dying, and they called us to the hospital. "Are you asking me or telling me?" she inquired. "Is your work complete? I need that report before you leave," she ordered.

Stricken with grief, I tried my best to get my work done, and as the hours were stripping away, I finally wrote a senior officer to tell them I was leaving. I packed my things up and left, just like that. I rushed home, packed some clothes, and sped down Interstate 95.

"How far are you away, Baby?" my mother asked.

"I will be there in about an hour," I replied.

Twenty minutes left in my drive; I got a call that my aunt had passed. I got to that hospital and collapsed into the arms of my mom, and cried from the depths of my soul. I hated my boss with every ounce of vile I could muster up. When I got back to work, I was so enraged and so bitter that I could barely see straight. Before my aunt died, I was on the radio talking about the toxic environment in which I now found myself working, but that was beyond toxic; it was sickening. Every time I saw her, smelled her perfume, felt the warmth of her body as she stood over me—micromanaging my work—I was getting closer and closer to quitting.

About a week after losing my aunt, a coworker lost her father, and the managers sent out a note and had the nerves to ask me for money. They stuck the dagger in deeper with, "Good thing is she was by his bedside when he died." I could not see straight. For the first time in my life, I did not care about money, status, job, career, or anything. I wanted out. I refused to engage in any pleasantries with that woman.

She later told me, "We just have to forgive and move on." I thought to myself; *I will never forgive you for what you did.* I wanted her to experience the pain and suffering I had gone through—not just her but all of them. I prayed many nights for all those involved in harming me. Each night, I asked God to vindicate me against them. One by one, I called their names out, finding some level of peace in knowing one day they would all reap a harvest for what they had done to me. I went into the office on January 27, 2014, determined I would not live another day working with that drama. I packed my things and took them to the car. Then I walked back into the office and handed her my resignation letter with a piece of my mind. "You are a terrible person and a horrible leader," I admitted. "I don't know what you did to get this job," I told her and left, just like that.

Before I went to that center, another lady at the company had called me crying on the phone with thirty-three years of service; she just up and quit. I tried to talk her out of it, but less than six months later, I joined her in leaving with no plan. If she dared to do it, so could I. The difference is she had a husband. I was single and labeled an "angry black woman." Yes, I was angry. I was angry because I loved my organization, and I let those two toxic leaders take me down. I know God warned me for it by sending me dreams and visions, but I vastly underestimated the pain and suffering I would experience. Roman 8:18-19 (NLT) states, Yet what we suffer now is nothing compared to the glory he will reveal to us later. For all creation is waiting eagerly for that future day when God will reveal who his children really are."

I quit that job with the intent of finally writing the book the Lord had told me to write, but my suffering was not over. My family was in deep sorrow because of our losses. Before we could bury one, we were burying another, and then another, and before it was all said and done, I lost seven close members of our family—one to gun violence—and my best friend's mother, whom I've known since I was a child. As if that was not enough, the man I loved had another woman all along whom he married and placed the wedding pictures on Facebook for the whole world to see.

I tried everything to get my life back on track, but each of those sorrows left me incapable of getting up on my own. I had stood with everyone in my family, using my event skills to plan or help plan a funeral. I thought I was doing the right thing by being there for everyone, but all it left me was broken and burned out. I emptied my bank account, loaned money I could not afford, and as a result, lost relationships that, at one point, meant the world to me. I also became a laughingstock as people thought I was foolish for leaving my job without an action plan. All I knew was I could not stay there, not with the bitterness I had in my heart toward my manager.

In retrospect, the eagle has always resonated with me. My fascination with birds started with my name meaning angelic messengers. Jumping out of the nest to soar to higher heights would have been great if I did not have so many fractures in my wings. I allowed the things that happened in my life to hinder my flight. I had all these spiritual words in me and had prayed for miracles to occur in other people's lives and saw them come to pass, but I could not find enough hope to believe God would do it for me. I had once prayed for someone to live with a zero chance of survival, and God answered my prayer and manifested a miracle. I saw Him moving in everyone's life but my own.

My world became dark as night. My inability to get a job right away left me penniless. My Mercedes got repossessed, my house was in foreclosure, I had no clothes, my ministry had dried up, I had no love life, my mother was in deep grief, and some of the friends I used to have deserted me. My life was so bad that I could not get up. Someone in my family told me, "We used to look up to you; you used to have it all." I felt like a gazingstock.

Years ago, an apostle gave me an utterance from the Lord before my world fell apart. He said to me, "Sister, I hope you don't get mad at me, but the Lord told me to give you this Word from Hebrews 10:32–36 (KJV):

> "But call to remembrance the former days, in which, after ye were illuminated, ye endured a great fight of afflictions; Partly, whilst ye were made a gazingstock both by reproaches and afflictions; and partly, whilst ye became companions of them that were so used. For ye had compassion of me in

> my bonds, and took joyfully the spoiling of your goods, knowing in yourselves that ye have in heaven a better and an enduring substance. Cast not away therefore your confidence, which hath great recompence of reward. For ye have need of patience, that, after ye have done the will of God, ye might receive the promise.

I received the word, but it was yet another reminder that I had not done the will of God, which was to write. I cannot tell you what the message would have been had I done what the Lord told me to do when He told me to do it, but I can tell you now I learned things about God, myself, and people I would have never known had I not gone through those dark times. When the spirit of offense makes its way into your heart, there is no way out but forgiveness, a journey I was not quite ready to tackle.

I attempted to write my book, but it read like a Blues record—a "somebody done me wrong" song. There was no power in it, no victory on the words of my pages. Frankly, when I first left my job, I noticed no one wanted to hear why I resigned. They did not care. All they knew was I left a lucrative career to sit on the back of my mother's deck, studying birds. I overheard someone ask my mom if I had lost my mind. I knew I did not, but I also knew I just could not go back to the life I had. The grudge I had against my manager was too big of a hurdle to overcome, in addition to a failed abusive relationship, which left me unable to move forward.

I can recall falling off a horse in the eighth grade and being afraid to get back on it. People tried to convince me to ride again, but I could not do it. As I look back, I understand why they wanted me to try again. Riding horses gives you such a sense of freedom. You and the horse are operating together as one; you become him, and he becomes you. The fear I had of hurting myself stopped me from trying again. Hitting the ground from a high place is a hurtful thing, and in many ways, losing my job and my relationship made me feel like I fell off the horse.

The leaders hurt me in my organization, the man I trusted and friends abandoned me—plus the lack of support I needed from those who meant the most to me—left me with scars, but all those lessons were good to learn. I sat on my mother's back deck, contemplating those things; life's realities were a constant reminder of my failure, and I fell right back into a "woe is me" mindset. The inability to shift from this thinking made me feel as if I had no real reason to live—as if life were over for me. I wanted to leave this earth. I tried hard to find a reason to stay here. Though I love my family, I was seemingly offending them, and they could not see past my failure. I could not hold my head up around them. I was convinced I was done with this world, but God had another plan for me.

My dear friend, Nicole, called me and heard the despair in my voice. I confessed to her that I was having thoughts of suicide, and she prayed for me. I sat on that phone and cried until my eyes began to swell. I thanked her for her obedience and found the strength to "run on," as the elders of my church would say—to see what the end will be. I lost someone I love very much to suicide, and the devastation it does to those left behind was nothing I wanted my family to experience. I had to fight for my life while drowning in an ocean of grief.

I decided to think about the time I had sitting with my elders, as talking to someone making their transition from earth to eternity is strangely beautiful. All their wisdom and life lessons from the view of hindsight are a once-in-a-lifetime opportunity to grow. As I began to glean from the fields of their experiences, I realized God was giving me a gift more valuable than silver and gold. He deposited treasure in me to one day distribute to all who had an ear to hear. Each one had something special to leave me.

After a while, I considered Peter—stepping out on faith to walk on water, to defy the very laws of gravity in the Gospel of Matthew. He did what no other disciple dared to do, but when he took his eyes off Jesus and began to see the winds and the waves, he began to sink. Even during that emergency, he had the presence of mind to call on the Lord, and He immediately saved him.

Matthew 14:25–31 (NLT)

> "About three o'clock in the morning Jesus came toward them, walking on the water. When the disciples saw him walking on the water, they were terrified. In their fear, they cried out, "It's a ghost!" But Jesus spoke to them at once. "Don't be afraid," he said. "Take courage. I am here![b]" Then Peter called to him, "Lord, if it's really you, tell me to come to you, walking on the water." "Yes, come," Jesus said. So Peter went over the side of the boat and walked on the water toward Jesus. But when he saw the strong[c] wind and the waves, he was terrified and began to sink. "Save me, Lord!" he shouted. Jesus immediately reached out and grabbed him. "You have so little faith," Jesus said. "Why did you doubt me?"

It was admirable for me to think I was acting like Peter by leaving my job—that or visions of grandeur.

Peter was radical in his faith, a sort of hot head, without much emotional intelligence (EI). In that regard, we had a lot in common, but the difference between Peter and me is he left the safety of his boat after consulting with the Lord. I left my job after an offense. I could not stand to look at my boss another day. He stepped out on faith. I stepped out on pride. We both failed miserably, and we both needed God to fix our situations. Mine just was not immediate because I had some lessons to learn.

In in college, I took a photography class and learned to develop film negatives in the darkroom. The excitement was seeing your picture come into fruition after applying just the right amount of time and chemical substances. A great negative meant a great picture; it's amazing how wisdom can be found in simple things. In hindsight, God allowed those negative situations to develop my character and my obedience. The Bible speaks about the great falling away that the church will experience in the last days. The things I saw in church, the hurts I experienced in my life, and my own pride and false expectations or understanding of true intimacy with God pushed me further away from Him. As I began to meditate on the wrongs in my life, I kept attracting more things to devastate my soul. I needed a change that would bring me out of the darkness and into His marvelous light, but it's always darkest just before dawn.

The Epiphany

"Arise, shine; for your light has come, and the glory of the Lord has risen upon you." —Isaiah 60:1 (KJV)

When I left my job, the world had changed. For most of my professional life, I worked at the same company. Applying and competing in a market saturated with resumes and recent college graduates was now a daunting task. The more closed doors I encountered, the more my self-esteem was diminishing. After my friend prayed for me, I decided to fast. For thirty days, I fasted—seventeen without food. I had to hear from God. I thought if I followed all the formulas of getting into His presence, He would open doors for me. It was no easy task, and I was hungry, but I was broke and needed a miracle fast. The thirteen cents in my bank account was not even enough for me to buy candy from the store.

Once I completed consecration, I expected God to tell me a word to change my life. I went to church anticipating a burning bush experience—a "take off your shoes for the place you are standing is holy" experience. Instead, the message was, "Don't give up on God because God won't give up on you?" *What? I am starving. That's it,* I thought to myself.

I was disappointed and annoyed I did not get a different message. Stomach growling and spirit grumbling, I left the church house with an attitude. *This doesn't work,* I thought. I told my friends about my experience, and all they could do was laugh. It wasn't funny to me because I wanted more than that. I wanted to hear one of those words that make you shout all over the church, the kind where you bask in His glory. Instead, I felt uninspired because I had given up on God, and I felt like He gave up on me.

All the utilities were off at my house, so I had to stay with my mom until I could get them reconnected. Walking by her daily with no motivation was frustrating to her because she was supporting me. She was unhappy, but she could not see me cold and hungry. I know I was grown, in my forties, but a mother's love transcends age. She never saw herself taking care of her adult child, but she always did what she had to do for her family..

I decided to get a job at a local salad restaurant. At least that was honest work. Standing in line, barely able to see through my old glasses, I attempted to make those salads. The heat from the lights was causing me to sweat, and my shirt was drenched, but I wanted to make a good impression. I also needed the money. The hat they gave me did not fit over my now long, loc'd hair, and the humiliation of sitting it on my head and tying my hair around it to stay on was a sight to behold. My feet also throbbed as I had not stood anywhere for eight hours since I was a young adult.

Lord, what have I done? I wondered. The young people were working circles around me, and I could not tell the difference between basil and cilantro. They were right next to each other, and I couldn't see past my fogged-up eyeglasses. I pulled them up over above my eyebrows and leaned in closer to see how to make one lady's salad and happened to catch a glimpse of how she was looking at me. This lady, in her fancy suit, saw me sweating over her salad, squinting my eyes, struggling to fix one of our signature dishes, and I wanted to fly away. If I had superpowers that day, I would have transported myself to another space in the universe, anywhere but there.

I could read her thoughts as I imagined her saying, "Lady, you don't know how to make a salad . . . as old as you are." I went home and told my mother, and she said slowly but with humor, "*I am sooo ashamed.*" My mother and sister laughed at that story until they cried; they even made me act it out for them. We all laughed, and I said, "I can't do this. What if someone from my previous job walked in and saw me?" I would have been the laughingstock of the whole organization, so I gave myself permission to only work there for two days. I was back at square one—broke, busted, and disgusted. Still, I had my pride, and I was not ready to give it to God.

When the Lord teaches us a lesson, location is irrelevant. It does not matter if you are in a salad place or an executive office; His desires lean toward obedience. Shortly after that, my friend suggested substitute teaching. I applied for and received my certificate to teach in public schools. This certificate boosted my motivation because at least I knew I could finally get paid. Going from self-reliance to dependency was the worst part of leaving my job. It's one thing to rely on the Lord for your daily bread; it's another to survive on the benevolence of others. Though I appreciated that my mother never made me feel unwelcome at her dinner table, I wanted so badly not to have to be there, so I gladly took the job.

I went to work at an elementary school in my neighborhood. I worked there for one week and was asked to become a long-term substitute. *What an easy job,* I thought. My first experience was with a Pre-K class. The children went to sleep at noon, and I was off work by 3:30 p.m. The Lord had a sense of humor because I quickly realized had He given me any other class that week, I would have left the building immediately.

Children are different now. As a society, I am not sure when we determined to put elders at the bottom of the food chain; however, children have created a merit-based system whereby an adult must earn the respect of younger people before receiving it. Mistreating people based on their age is like sparking a fire in a library of historic literary masterpieces. For every wrinkle, every gray hair, every slow step, there is a story to pass on to the next generation, much like passing the baton in track.

Maybe we have allowed this to happen in our society because we did not like correction growing up, so we determined we would change things for the next generation. I hear parents say, "I'm going to give my children everything I did not have," but often, that translates to forgetting to give them what they did have. I see shoes, clothes, no curfew, phones, unearned money, shut doors in houses, and even unreasonable demands. I rarely see respect, responsibility, accountability, discipline, and boundaries. This behavior is reflected in television programming created for children. Animations, movies, and sitcoms spotlight children slamming doors in parents' faces, yelling at them, walking off while they are talking, rolling their eyes, and being disrespectful.

How could any child, learning to process their emotions, navigate the hierarchies of life while watching that type of programming and not think it's acceptable behavior? Their brains have been "programmed" to relate to expressing their anger to adults in an aggressive manner. Since this is not my family's culture, I did not know what I was about to experience as a substitute teacher.

My strong background in human resources prepared me to deal with people. I was astonished to learn the same bullying behavior, lack of interpersonal skills, dignity, and respect I saw over the years working with adults is the same behavior I saw in children. The adults were still bullies. Instead of taking lunch money, they take mortgages, car notes, and food off the table of hard-working employees.

The first time I attempted to control a class, I failed miserably. I was grossly unprepared to be told, "Shut up, B-Word." I was utterly shocked. I wondered how I could possibly survive a job where the children were verbally abusing adults. To me, I had hit rock bottom. A child calling you an expletive and being powerless to do anything about it was as low as I had ever been. Unfortunately, I could not leave the job because I needed the money. I stuck it out but barely made it through the semester. The following year I took a long-term assignment as an art teacher. It's art; what's the worst thing that can happen? *Insert shock emoji here!* There is plenty that could go wrong in an art class (i.e., Crayon wars!).

As it turned out, teaching art was the most challenging and rewarding job I had ever had. Art should never be taken out of the school curriculum. What the students could not communicate verbally, they expressed through art. The use of colors, shapes, and imagery often showed the deep pain suffered by the artist. Vincent van Gogh painted the famous picture, *Starry Night*, from an asylum.

Many of my students drew images of death, sorrow, and violence. It was hard to see a third grader draw a picture with a gun, killing someone. Though the money was not the same as my former job, I realized God had allowed me to be there to love those children, and my heart was big enough to accept all of them. Some could not focus on the imagination assignments and often asked me to give them another sheet after they messed up. "Create from your mistakes," I would say. I was talking to them, but I was also ministering to myself, unaware.

I had made some mistakes in my life. I left my job without a plan, and I stayed in my relationship way too long. I was on a journey, and God used art to help me find my way back to Him and back to me. Before each class, I printed a maze and asked each class to get out of it. The older students received more challenging mazes. During one class, one of my most closed students was frustrated at his inability to find his way out of his maze, shaped like a knight on a horse. He balled the paper up and threw it away, and instantly got angry with me. Lovingly, I talked to him about his dream of being a firefighter.

"Imagine you are the firefighter, and you are also the person stuck in the fire. What would you want you to do to get you out of the burning building? Would you want you to give up and throw in the towel like you just did, or would you want you to find a way to save you?"

"I would want me to save me," he replied.

"Then take this sheet of paper and save yourself."

I gave him the paper, and I sat with him for moral support. It took him a while, but he found his way out. He looked at me and said, "I did it!" I told him if he could find his way out this maze, then he can find his way out of any situation in life." I became his favorite teacher from that moment. Many of my students may have started disrespecting me, but I kept coming back. I served them with a heart of love, and they gave it back to me.

Once that assignment ended, I had to teach math. I made the students create a business and use basic math to tell me what they would do with the money. They had to add, subtract, multiply, divide, and use percentages. One student told me he didn't need this lesson because he was going to the NFL. "Oh, really," I said. "Okay, I'm going to do your assignment on the board."

I gave him an optional contract for five million dollars over five years. I knew he did not read it, so we went directly to spending money. He brought a house for his mother, himself, a fancy car, expensive jewelry, took care of his entourage, and had lots of parties. He got hurt his rookie year and missed ten games, which caused him to go to a $250,000 fixed salary, and he failed to pay the IRS. When we finished that lesson, he owed more money than he was making. The look on his face was hilarious as he said, "Wait, how did I become broke?" The entire class was laughing. I asked him if he learned anything from the lesson, and he said he would pay attention in class and learn how to manage his money.

Those life lessons made me feel like I had tapped into something purposeful. People talk about low-income people as if they have no redeeming qualities. That is furthest from the truth. When a child who has suffered a lack in any area finally discovers the key to wellness, they receive it with gladness. I worked at that job until I got an opportunity I could not resist. I had an assignment request for the Duke Ellington School of the Arts. When I noticed they needed a substitute teacher, I was more than thrilled to split my time between both schools. I did not expect to be so overwhelmed with emotion when I got there.

As a teenager, the school I wanted to attend had a dedicated public bus I could catch from the local subway to the school's front doors. As a guest teacher, I could ride the bus designated for students. I could not believe this bus went directly past my childhood home. It picked up students at the same stop; I would have been at; I wondered what was happening in that instance. I felt like I was in a time machine, where I would see where my life would be if I had stepped out on faith and gone to the school despite our financial situation.

My life was in shambles; I only made $120 a day, yet, I met my tribe at that school. All my life, I had been searching for meaning. I often felt like a misfit. When I saw those students, I instantly understood myself like never before. I was a creative soul. I was trying to fit into a corporate world where I did not belong, at least not as an employee.

Throughout the halls, students had color in their hair, dirty Converse, or homemade clothes. They marched to the beat of their own tune. They were writers, visual artists, singers, musicians, actors, dancers, museum curators, photographers, set designers, and so forth. They were all unique but had one thing in common: they were dreamers. Seeing those young people commit to their craft was convicting to me. They breathed their dreams. They often were rejected by their local peers but found solace in each other. They understood the grind. The school had workshops and kept them exposed to stars. They were never led to believe following your dreams would be easy, but they followed anyway.

Each time I saw the students perform, a wave of inspiration came over me. This could have been me had I dared to live the life I wanted. I was approaching fifty years old and was suffocating in the quest to pay my bills. Maybe I was having a midlife crisis; perhaps I was waking up. Whatever the reason, I felt God had led me there to see what I could've achieved had I trusted Him.

I had to teach a class about August Wilson's play, *Fences*. In this class, we entered a discussion about literal fences. In facilitating this class and talking to the brilliant students, I realized fences have two purposes: to keep things in and to keep things out. They can be created using many materials; the stronger the material, the more fortified the structure. My fence was made of bricks. All the years of offenses had kept love from coming in and going out. There were cracks in my wall, but either way, my fence served as a prison to keep me bound. My warden was unforgiveness, and my chains were pride. I was too proud to forgive those who hurt me, and though I had the key and wanted to be set free, I did not know how to use it, so I sat there, watching young people fulfill their dreams while I only thought about mine.

The Lord was gracious enough to allow me to get my utilities turned back on, and I liked having the flexibility to work as a substitute teacher. Still, it was not enough money to pay my bills, and I did not have benefits, so I had to think about living like an adult with responsibilities. Once again, I began to hunt for a job. I finally landed a position at a school in Maryland as a registrar. I thought my years as a secretary and project manager would make this job easy for me, but it wasn't. The complexities of this role and being an external hire, filling the position of someone who had been there for thirty years, did not make me popular.

My first thoughts were to immediately discover how to improve the chaos presented to me in the front office. As a new hire with no understanding of the policies and no time to get up to speed, I was stepping on the toes of those who did not agree with my being hired. I was also frustrating the people waiting for me to understand my job, all during the first weeks of school. The rocky start created an atmosphere of tension and mistrust. *Here we go again,* I thought. *Lord why? I need to work. I just want to do meaningful work and go home and enjoy my life. How is the same trial coming back to me? Maybe my ex-manager was right. We don't get to like our jobs*. That's what she told me as she made sure I did not like mine.

My previous life's stressors had landed me in the doctor's office, with a blood pressure of 203/102. I was not living my best life, and this new job did not help. The medicine I was given helped control my blood pressure, but it did nothing for my motivation. I wanted to go back to Duke Ellington, where at least I felt welcomed. My mother, seeing my dilemma, offered me a sound piece of advice. "Ann, you have great ideas. You are smart and capable of doing a good job, but you are like a bull in a china cabinet. I know you want to see change, but not having any experience with that job and telling them what needs to be fixed is not working for you. Change must come softly sometimes, Baby. Show them, don't tell them, and let them see your good works."

This was the only thing that kept me from leaving that job. Ironically, when my mother was a young girl, bulls fascinated her. One day she convinced her brothers to go with her to play matador with a bull. She took a red shirt and waved it at the bull until it went mad. This bull got out, and it took several men to contain it. It was the talk of the whole town.

My grandfather did not understand why the bull went mad like that, but my mother knew. For years, she held the shame of her mischievous actions. Her respect for her father was at such a level that she confessed it when she became an adult. He was disappointed, but his love for my mom allowed him to offer her grace. I saw myself going through my life knocking things down like that angry bull in her story, but the softness of my mother's words calmed me.

I took her advice and began to do things differently at work. My customers became my primary focus. I loved them, and they loved me. We built a great relationship, and I did not know how much I would need my customers until I got a dreaded phone call from my mother. "Baby, the cancer has come back in stage 4," she said. The doctors had given her one year to live. It was as if someone had knocked the breath out of me.

My mother dying topped all the hell I had gone through in my life. How could God do such a thing?

It was at that point that I drifted further away from Him emotionally. I was numb. Laughter filled my mother's last year on earth. She lived like she was dying and enjoyed the moments given to her. On the other hand, I felt lonelier than I ever had in my life. When I quit my job, I got a Shih Tzu/Pomeranian mixed-breed puppy born with a heart in her fur. I named her "The Fabulous Ruby Dee." She was heaven-sent to me. Were it not for her when the reality of my mother's death hit, I honestly don't think I could have withstood the pain.

My dog slept by me, sat at my feet, huddled on me when I cried, and provided the love of God to me in the form of an animal. Being single in the house, suffering from grief, was a recipe for disaster. I was not making it. My best friend, Darlene, advised me to get counseling, and it was the best decision of my life. It helped me to see my worth, begin healing from my past, and encourage me to rewrite my life's scripts. Talking to the counselor opened me up enough to finally forgive those who hurt me. I even received an apology and forgave the man I wanted to marry because he deserves forgiveness and mercy just like I do. Sometimes in church, people advise you to fake it until you make it. In therapy, it was about being real by getting to the root cause of your problem and letting God take it out of your soul (mind, will, emotions). Amos 2:9 (NLT) teaches, "But as my people watched, I destroyed the Amorites though they were as tall as cedars and as strong as oaks. I destroyed the fruit on their branches and dug out their roots."

Therapy has such a bad stigma. We go through life experiencing trauma in our relationships, in our families, at our jobs, in our finances, even just by listening to the news. We take that trauma, even subconsciously, with us wherever we go. I have had single mothers threaten to harm me at work for just doing my job. I have seen people display road rage and have watched families break up because of other people's brokenness. We cannot go on like this as a society. We must get help. These broken people lead industries, start families, teach our children, drive our buses, and shape our minds—even preach in our churches. This world is fallen, but we have a Savior, and through His Words, we find comfort and answers to our problems.

My broken bosses, unfaithful partners, mean kids, bad decisions, and more broke me. I had dreams of doing great things; I wanted to do them, but I could not get off the ground to fly. As my mother began her transition from earth to the presence of the Lord, she called me phenomenal. At Bennett College, they endeavored to produce phenomenal women. Ms. Maya Angelou's poem, "Phenomenal Woman," was indeed part of our mantra. The woman I thought I was disappointing gave me enough encouragement in those words to want to do better with my life.

After she passed in November, I went to work in December and received a glass figurine inscribed, "The love of family is the greatest gift of all." I accidentally dropped the bag it was in, and the glass broke. A coworker said, "It's shattered; you will never put that back together again." Something about those words pierced my heart. I thought, *the devil is a liar.*

I researched "putting glass back together" purchased some glass glue. I gave the base a new foundation and used tweezers to fix it as best I could. Where there were pieces that could no longer fit, I replaced them with Venetian glass pieces. When I showed them what I did, they could not believe it. I know it was just words about broken glass, but to me, those words reflected my life and my family, and I did not like hearing "It could not be put back together again." I spent the Christmas holiday looking at that glass, studying what I had just done, and wanted the same thing for myself—for my family—and just like that glass, I had to replace some things. To be honest, I did not know what those things were going to be, so I went back to my daily schedule.

Going back to work under the same pressure while dealing with grief was hard for me. The year 2020 was going to be a year of restoration, a year of Jubilee, but working at the job under stressful conditions made my healing difficult. On March 17, 2020, we were told our school was closing because of a global pandemic. The world was turned upside down by COVID-19, the virus five times more deadly than the flu. Our country shut down, and other single people and I were locked in our homes by ourselves. Lonely and depressed, I sat in my house and fed my emotions. I was reluctant to get on the scale but felt I had to. When I did, I was astonished at my weight. I was 237 pounds. I was larger than I had ever been. That, for me, was the last straw.

I came into this world born at 2:37 a.m. one beautiful autumn day, and I was reborn in the summer of 2020 when I got on a scale and weighed 237 pounds. It hit me like a bolt of lightning—my "ah-ha" moment. Nobody was coming to save me but me. Jesus had already paid the price for my sins. I am forgiven, but I had a part to play in the story of my life. I did not know how to fix my problems. My spirit was willing, but my flesh was weak. I went to YouTube and heard a message from the late Bishop G. E. Patterson entitled "Discouraged." *That's it, Lord,* I thought. *I'm discouraged. I have lost confidence in Your willingness to fix my situation.*

I went upstairs to my prayer room and confessed my sins and flaws. I humbly asked the Lord to make me whole—spirit, soul, body, financially, and socially. I began to pray, "You were wounded for my transgressions and bruised for my iniquities. The chastisement of my peace was on You, and by Your stripes, I am healed." I then opened my great-grandmother's Bible, and it fell to the words of Jesus, "Woman, thou art loosed from thine infirmity." I got so excited because I knew that was my Word from God, the Word I had been waiting to hear for seven years. I cut my spiritual teeth listening to the "Woman Thou Art Loosed" message from Bishop T. D. Jakes. God took me back to the place where I first believed, an answer to my prayer.

I got up, and my life changed from that moment. I realized I needed help in the physical realm, so I assembled my buffalos. In the animal kingdom, buffalos surround a wounded herd member if a lion tries to devour it. 1st Peter 5:8 (NLT) tells us, "Stay alert! Watch out for your great enemy, the devil. He prowls around like a roaring lion, looking for someone to devour." The buffalo will stand with you until it's no longer advantageous for the enemy. My Buffalo Soldiers, as I so affectionately call them, have been my concrete support. They have made sure I lacked for nothing. They helped me get back up.

With a new perspective and a greater outlook on life, I joined the National Novel Writing Month Camp in July 2020. Finally, I did what the Lord had required of me. Halfway through my book, I received a job offer! I had finally found my place. It was a nonprofit organization whose mission of advancing a more equitable city through the lens of food, education, and opportunity was in line with my values. They did not believe in only helping people survive crises; they promoted thriving. I went from hating my job and dealing with all the heartache that came from dreading going to work to loving my job and being extremely grateful I was chosen to work at a company where I could find joy in my work. It wasn't about money, fame, or any type of status; it was about living life on purpose.

In my new role, I became a coach, a partner of equity, a carrier of love, and an advocate of change—a collection of all the things I needed myself when life had gotten the best of me. As I connected to my community and contemplated life's mysteries, I evolved into another version of me: a servant of God's love, redemption, mercy, and empathy. My new company even sent me to Trinity Washington University to get my Master of Science in Administration focusing on Dynamic Leaders and Organizations. When interviewed, I was asked, "Why do you want to work here?" I told them because some people are born to sing, I was born to serve. To that end, it is my sincere desire that this book finds itself in the hands of people who have lost hope—even to the brink of suicide. It can get better; hold on and seek professional help, my brother and my sister. You can dream again for the ones with broken dreams; you must take the time to heal.

To the people in abusive relationships, after I got my new job, I asked God, "Now, why would I want to be with a man who makes me cry when you make me smile?" Learning to love yourself will make room for the divine love you desire. Though I still wait for it to happen to me, I also realize the journey to self-love can be long when you've spent so many years off the beaten path. To the people grieving, weeping may endure for a night, but joy cometh in the morning. For the Christian who lost their way, I'm sorry those things happened to you. I know you may blame God in your reasoning, but He loves you with an everlasting love.

When I was at my lowest, I had a "Why bother the Master mentality." That's not how God feels about His children. He misses you, and He wants you to come back home. There's a fatted calf, a signet ring, and a robe waiting just for you. For seven years, I walked away from God as a prodigal child. I thought, as I had been told, that I would never get back on my feet or get out of financial trouble. My lack of adequate income resulted in foreclosure, and I was tremendously afraid of being homeless. But in the nick of time, right before my house was going to finally be auctioned, I qualified for a modification after fighting and praying for years.

Every seed I had sown in my community had finally come back to me in an abundance of favor, and I will spend the rest of my life as a healer, advocate, humanitarian, and philanthropist for those whose wings are too broken to fly. If you are reading this and think God is not real, there are no coincidences. This is a seed of faith, and just like that apple seed I planted when I was young, I believe your faith will grow, and when you are converted, go strengthen your brethren.

Life Lessons Learned from My Great Cloud of Witnesses

I gleaned pearls of wisdom from all my elders. For instance, I learned never to forget my roots from the uncle who moved away from home but always came back. From another, I marvel at the lessons of working with the heart of love as I reflected on my elder's passion for his work. As a bus driver, he found purpose in helping people get to their destination. He also made me promise him that I would one day preach the Gospel as I ministered the Word of God to him after he got sick.

Lest I forget the lessons learned from my impeccably dressed uncle as he insisted that I need to work on "keeping my cool" when among great people. He would tell me, "Always K. I. T. (Keep It Together), Niecy Piecy." He felt I needed to know this after meeting a handsome actor and losing the intellect of conversation around him. Though he was a well-put-together man, his love for his family was evident in all that he did. He did not exclude anyone, and he felt his life passion was to bring people together for good food, laughter, and solidarity. He recognized that the family and community are strongest when we stand together. No matter how many problems we faced as a family, he was a peacemaker. We would not have survived after my grandparents died without his insisting that we make each other a priority. He told us it was a "God mission," and he spent his last years answering the call to unite our family.

My beautiful aunt praised God during her worst storms; she never lost gratitude or her praise. She had high hopes for me and rebuked me sharply when she found out I was still in my emotionally abusive relationship. Though she was suffering, she helped me see the importance of not allowing people to mistreat you. She knew I had a voice, and she wanted me to use it. She went through many hard things in her life, but she learned the divine order of love. You love God, you love yourself, and then you love others, the lesson in which I had to work the hardest on practicing. Spending the last days with her impacted my life, but I knew I had to listen when she challenged my relationship. She was not concerned about what I thought about it; she spoke truth to power in the spirit of love and genuine concern for me. I knew this woman loved me because after she finished telling me about her journey of love, I still had my dignity even though I knew I was settling for less than I was worth. In the last few years of her life, she experienced true love. After years of it not being right, love found her and supported her until her death. Her graciousness was known throughout her small town. As an educator, she was a friend to people in high places and humble beginnings. She was a gracious woman and indeed was the light of the world and the salt of the earth.

My adventurous aunt was always on the road. She did not get married until she was in her fifties. I always saw her as a bird. If she wanted something, she got it. This classy lady took fancy trips, had nice cars, and wore fine clothes. During her last days on earth, I spent time with her at her home in Fayetteville, NC. I went to her backyard, and she had a Zen garden back there with different kinds of trees, flowers, plants, and even a pond full of fish. As I was back there, taking it all in, I noticed she had Asian inscribed words on the stones. I asked her about them, and she asked where they were. I showed her the words Love, Prosperity, Hope, Trust, all in the yard, and she did not even realize it was back there. I asked, "How did you not see this?" She never spent a lot of time back there, so she did not notice what was in her garden. I told her, "Auntie, your backyard is very expensive." She said that's what the previous owner said when they bought the house. I told her, "You have to learn to slow down and stop and smell the roses." We spent a lot of time laughing and talking and decided to plant some flowers together, one of which was the forget-me-not flower, but she passed away before we could do so. In one of our conversations, I realized you can have everything you have ever wanted and nothing you need in life. I planted those flowers in my yard to honor that lesson because I was always asking God for my wants, but I had no clue what I needed.

My uncle, who was also my best friend, was a man who kept his word. If he told you he would do something, he did it. I could confide in him and share my deepest thoughts, and never once did he betray me. He was slow to speak but full of wisdom. I used to call him the family owl.

I knew I needed to learn this lesson from him. As a loquacious child, I could not stop talking, but he helped me understand its best to learn the art of silence—the time to speak and reframe from speaking. My life was filled with those teachable moments, but none more prevalent than being quiet when I should have spoken up for myself, which contributed to my hardship. Having the wisdom to speak the truth in love, without fear, can only come when you are quiet enough to hear from God to allow Him to season your words with salt when the need arrives for you to speak your truth.

My best friend's mother taught me about hospitality and keeping your sense of humor. Whenever I visited her, though she was ill, she made me laugh until I cried. She was a great mother who always had a hot meal for her children. I never went to her house without smelling something good cooking. It was always a pleasure to be in her presence. She made you feel like you were home, and she gave birth to a beautiful soul and the best friend a girl could ever have.

My first cousin, the man who protected me in high school and with whom I shared a crib, taught me about support. When I left my job, he paid for my cellphone bill and never made me feel bad about my decision to leave. When he passed, his daughter took on my cellphone bill, and his wife bought me clothes and supported me as much she could, even in her lack, because she said her husband loved me and would have wanted her to look after me.

My other cousin taught me about being courageous enough to do it alone. She moved to the Virgin Islands without family. I always thought that took a lot of courage.

My precious aunt and her husband of 58 years taught me about living off the land's harvest. I learned to fish and appreciate farm life.

Finally, my beautiful mother taught me how to pray and be strong. The pain of losing her has been a painful hurdle to overcome, but courageously I take the lessons she taught me about God and count them as the most valuable gems I had ever received, which I wear proudly.

CPSIA information can be obtained
at www.ICGtesting.com
Printed in the USA
BVHW071743190422
634466BV00002B/7

9 781662 845611